52 FAVOURITE WEST SUSSEX WALKS

Maps by Richard Williamson

Decorations by Debbie Powell

Summersdale Publishers Ltd
46 West Street
Chichester
West Sussex
PO19 1RP
UK

www.summersdale.com

Printed and bound in the Czech Republic

ISBN: 978-1-84953-233-4

Substantial discounts on bulk quantities of Summersdale books are available to corporations, professional associations and other organisations. For details contact Summersdale Publishers by telephone: +44 (0) 1243 771107, fax: +44 (0) 1243 786300 or email: nicky@summersdale.com.

52
Favourite
West Sussex
Walks

52
Favourite
West Sussex
Walks

Richard Williamson

summersdale

West Sussex

HOLLYCOMBE

FALLOW DEER

41

52 ROGATE COMMON

9

7 **48**

HENLEY COMM

MIDHURST

PETERSFIELD

46 **6**

51 SOUTH HARTING

S DW

COCKING

18 Q.E. FOREST

15

UPPARK

49 **20** EAST D

42

17

WEST DEAN WOODS

47

23 **38** **40**

50

WEST DEAN TRUNDLE

HAVANT FOREST

STANSTED FOREST

14

GOODWOOD

13

8

KINGLEY VALE

RIVER LAVANT

22

1

A.27

PEREGRINE

36

29 **26** SNIPE

31 CHICHESTER

THORNEY ISLAND

28 **27**

PILSEY ISLAND EAST HEAD

REDSHANK

HAYLING ISLAND

TEAL

WITTERINGS

34

37

PAGHAM HARBOUR

BRENT GEESE

BRACKLESHAM BAY

CHURCH NORTON

SAILORS GALORE

SELSEY

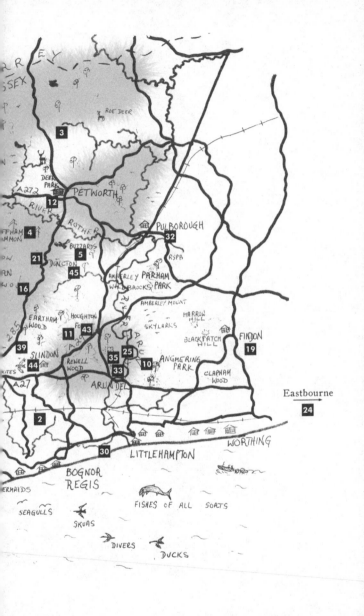

Contents

Downland Walks

Waterside Walks

Woodland Walks

Village Walks

Introduction

Here are fifty-two of my favourite walks through the beautiful county of West Sussex; I have travelled the world and can think of no finer place to be on the planet. There is so much to see around us: these walks open the door to the downs, estuaries, river valleys, woods, moors, marshes and mudflats down on the coast. We are not just walking; we are looking at the detail of the countryside around us and enriching our lives by admiring its complexity.

In these pages I'll show you where to find wild orchids, hear the song of the nightjar and stroll beneath the greatest oak trees in the land.

Together we will stride along the seawalls to watch the wild geese of winter and see the vast flocks of wading birds as they wheel in ever-changing shapes against the sunset. We will wander into the reed beds to hear the soothing, gentle susurration of the wind as it whispers with the flowing tide.

In the spring we can walk the ways through the coppice woods and see countless wild daffodils turning the woods bright yellow in the morning sun. Here we can listen for the spring call of the cuckoo and the nightingale, the song thrush and the garden warbler. Three hundred different species of wild flowers can be yours to view along the tracks and woodland paths which wind through the weald, which was once the dark and frightening forest of Anderida.

With my walk maps we can search for the tombs of ancient ancestors of the Bronze Age, scattered across the county; we can hunt the hilltops for the old mines where flints were extracted and broken up into usable tools such as axe and arrowheads, scrapers, hammers and knives – each tool had its own particular purpose. They are all there to be discovered. We can examine the hilltop forts of the Neolithic people of 8,000 years ago, and those of the Iron Age just before the Romans arrived.

My walks will also take you along the shingle banks of the coast, where we can look at unusual flowers that grow only there, and watch for sea ducks and terns that pass by on migration. Wherever possible I describe the little village churches on our route: each is individual and contains its own detail of life over 1,000 years of Christian culture. We can wander along the banks of the Rother and the Arun, enjoying the slow and sinuous curves, and hear the call of snipe and lapwing as they plunge in springtime flight about the meadows of the Wild Brooks.

Best of all, perhaps, we can soar like an eagle above the county along the crest of the Downs at Harting or Amberley, and see the buzzard gliding around us or watch the flocks of house martins swooping through the air as they gather for the flight south in the autumn. These Downs also have 300 species of wild flowers to enjoy, forming the centuries-old springy turf you can feel beneath your feet. On another day we can enter the ancient forest of 30,000 yew trees at Kingley Vale, the finest yew forest in Europe, or stroll along the ancient drove-ways where flocks of sheep were herded in centuries past.

With me on each journey, as ever, is my trusty white Morris Traveller, which acts as the start/finish marker on the maps and gets an honorary mention at the close of each walk. To assist in orientation I have provided Ordnance Survey grid references in the standard form – and although, for the most part, the walks are simple and straightforward, it is recommended that walkers provide themselves with appropriate Ordnance Survey maps, sensible clothing and a mobile telephone in case of emergency.

There is so much to see, so put me in your pocket and get walking now!

Common,
Farmland &
Heath Walks

Brandy Hole Copse

Its proximity to Chichester makes this an accessible and favourite walk for Cicestrians, its total distance being 4 km (2.5 miles).

I actually start from the Lavant end of the route; you can park at the roadside on Hunters Race, off the A286 on the Chichester side of Lavant at SU853076, and enter the Hunters Race meadow through the slipway in the hedge. The meadow was once a gravel pit, now grassed and planted with thousands of cowslips. Cross the circular mounds to admire the sculptures of iron men made of gas bottles, situated on

Centurion Way, which was the route of the old railway line. Fair numbers of herbs and flowers can be found along the way, which include teasel, comfrey, hardhead, and ox-eye daisies.

The walkway south is paved; best taken in with afternoon sunshine, when a few woodland butterflies may join you. There are also good numbers of woodland birds all the way around this walk, including blackbirds, robins, great tits, great spotted woodpeckers and a rookery. Large trees of sycamore, oak, holm oak, ash and lime line the way, and bramble and hawthorn blossoms attract butterflies. Passing under the road bridge, note the blackened brickwork above from the last sugar-beet trains up to 1991 (the passenger service was stopped in 1935). This is another access point from the north end of Chichester.

Next, turn right into **Brandy Hole Copse Local Nature Reserve**. This is partly funded by nine different agencies, including the RSPB and Wildlife Trusts, and is run by the Friends of Brandy Hole Copse, who do all the voluntary work of warden duties and management. They have done a wonderful job and need lots of help, so consider joining them if you can. Here you will tour their reserve, following the 2,000-year-old fortification bank built by late Iron Age people to protect their land from unfriendly tribes and Romans invading from north. This is known as Devil's Ditch and runs for 6 miles from Halnaker to West Stoke. It involved 110,000 tons of gravel movement. Here you will pass 'dragon's teeth' used in World War Two, which fortified Sussex from invasion from the south. I usually walk clockwise through the chestnut coppice, enjoying the bluebells and honeysuckle, then on to the two splendid woodland pools that are home to moorhens and kingcups.

Follow the ditch back east, enjoying the remarkable lofty trees as you go, some of which toppled in the hurricane of 1987. On the walk back along the previous route you should make a diversion at the road bridge, a little farther east, to see the third woodland pond tucked away here; another true delight, as is the return back along Centurion Way to the Minotaur, which would have put the wind up the Romans and the Ancient Brits.

The Morris awaits, hidden behind the hedge, glad of my return.

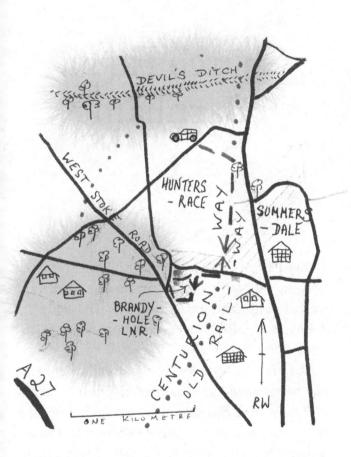

Church Farm, Barnham

Beware: this walk crosses a railway line with fast-moving trains, so if you have any hearing impairment take extra caution. The walk is 7 km (4.4 miles), over farmland with thick hedges and reedy rifes.

Parking can be found in the overflow church car park, amid the buildings of Church Farm, 600 m south of **Barnham station** at SU956035. You must then visit St Mary's Church and leave a donation. The 'white cap' tower of the church acts like a focal point during much of the walk. Look for the stone Tudor rose on the eastern outside wall of the church. Inside it looks like a splendid rose-coloured barn with two small Norman windows on the south side. There's lots of history to be seen even before you start this walk along the 1820s canal that once connected Chichester to London. A pink-painted swing bridge beams on display as you step westward along the curving banks of the old towpath.

A small patch of woodland will appear at the rail crossing: listen out first and be sharp in crossing the track. The trains are frequent and appear unexpectedly around the corners. Carry on down the old canal between newly planted hedges of oak and field maple on the right, with much yellow fleabane growing in season, and bristly ox-tongue at the far end. Passing the sewage works, note pied wagtails feeding on the sewage filter beds. A hundred metres after the last building, turn left down some steps, walking south across the meadows, looking out for the moorhens in the pools. Go half right along the sycamores and then, by a thick hedge, cross the stile into a meadow of Yorkshire fog grass.

Once you've arrived at Sack Lane, turn left, noting several 'dead' tractors, one a T21 Fordson. Walk straight through Lidsey Lodge

Farm and into the driftway, through a metal gate, where you'll find white bindweed (ladies' petticoats). Turn right along the muddy cows' walkway, then under some power cables. After about 200 m, cross left, diagonally, through a new fence: cross the railway again, taking the same care, noting the common horsetail growing around stones. Head south-east for a single pointed fir, then over the footbridge and turn half left, to the left of two fingerposts, finding a green metal footbridge over Lidsey Rife, and so on to Bognor golf course. Cross the greens north-east, to the footbridge with an old dogwood bush next to it. Turn sharply right to follow a hedge in a right-hand curve, but look left for a trig point hidden in bushes.

Take the next fingerposts pointing left, back under the power cables, following a rife. Cross the next footbridge, go left then right and follow the new yellow stone path back to canal – and on to the white cap, chatting to the white Morris.

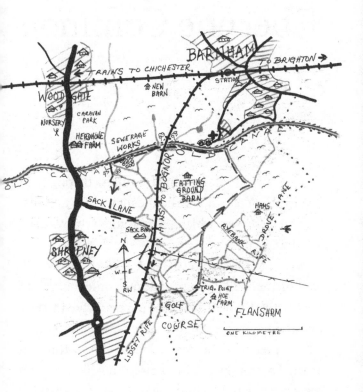

Ebernoe Common

Here is a walk of 2.6 km (1.6 miles) through the lovely Wealden woods and meadows of a national nature reserve, which is managed by Sussex Wildlife Trust.

Park at Holy Trinity Chapel SU976278, east of the A283, almost 5 km (3 miles) north of Petworth. Built in 1867, the chapel is beautifully maintained, with quixotic brickwork and a pure white interior. The east window shows thirteen at the Last Supper, Christ risen, holding orb and sceptre, angels adoring; the west window displays a fine design of vines. Kneelers show wild flowers: note number seven, which shows fritillaries. The churchyard is famous for its 120 species of plants:

dozens of spotted orchids and some large teasels by the south door when I visited in June.

Next walk south, down to fifteenth-century **Furnace Pond**. Herons and grebes can be spotted here. Follow the trail back uphill as it curves left then, coming to a cattle grid and interpretative board, turn right at the fingerpost. The track climbs a little to a grove of very large and spectacular old beech and oak trees; some have bat boxes attached to help conserve the fourteen separate species of the sixteen found in the UK. You'll find dead wood on left, deposited to help support the fungi (1,000 species of fungi have been named in this wood) and also for the beetles, whose larvae feed on the carbohydrates released when the wood decomposes. Among the beetles you may see in summer is the cardinal beetle, rich cardinal-red in colour – a colour seen in Renaissance paintings of elevated clergymen. There are also many species of wasps, bees and ichneumon that depend on dead wood – a very valuable habitat.

The woodlands are also home to butterflies such as the purple emperor, the white admiral and the silver-washed fritillary. You will certainly see speckled woods all through the summer on this wide, grassy ride. The track then descends through hazel and oak coppice where dormice might live. Robins and wrens, marsh tits and long-tailed tits are common here, as are woodpeckers and owls.

As you descend to a boggy area with willows, look for a right turn on a fingerpost. Next, cross a lovely buttercup meadow, with sheep sorrel, hardhead, and stitchwort. You will arrive at some woodland, where you'll see a broken stile: note the fallen beech-root plate on your right, under which grows yellow pimpernel.

Step down the bluebell bank to the bog below – the footbridges should get you across. Walk up the other side to find various woodland plantings of hazel coppice, Scots pine and chestnut coppice; look out for hard ferns in ditches. Tall oaks will greet you as you come to the minor road where you should turn right, first noting a small patch of wood mellick grass under the gate. The road here takes you back through quintessential English countryside and through the middle of a village cricket pitch. You can't get more eccentric than that, unless you drive an old Morris like mine through the deep field and catch a boundary four off a googly on the way.

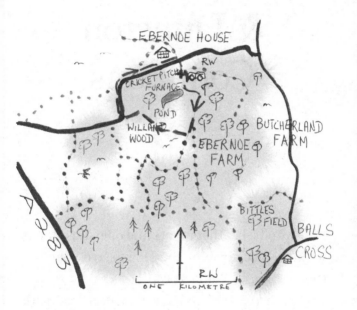

Lavington
& Duncton
Commons

Pine woods, heather moors and open farmlands with the backdrop of the Downs are yours on this 6.2 km (3.9 miles) walk.

Start at the National Trust roadside car park at SU949187 – the car park is not easy to find, being just north of a line between Graffham and Duncton. The small display panel tells you about hobby falcons, stonechats and sundews. Walk east past this, onto a track through ling and bell heather. Note that pines have been left here and there for the hobby falcons to breed, because they like clumps rather than solid woodland. Having crossed the open area, you'll come to a stile (but no fence) where you should turn left, with a long rhododendron hedge on your left. After 250 m, turn right onto a long straight ride through some lovely tall Scots pines – no arrows to be followed yet. Woodpeckers, great tits, blackbirds, all calling.

After 700 m, while going downhill with holly bushes around, you'll come to a gorse bush where you should follow the yellow arrow route right, keeping a large dead oak behind you. Continue straight over the footpath crossway, then after about 200 m going downhill you will come to a footbridge over a small stream – mind the holes in the floorboards here. Walking up the other side, turn right on the yellow arrow route – 40 m along this path note a holly bush on the left used as a scent stock by a roebuck. Soon after you should turn sharply left on the yellow arrow route and, after 29 m, you'll see that the path forks: take the right fork and you will eventually arrive at the road where Herringbroom Cottages have fine barge boards. Cross this road, with the magnificence of the wooded downland escarpment stretched ahead of you. The footpath then runs 900 m south-east over farm fields towards the Catholic church of St Anthony & St George. You can stop for lunch here, sitting among the primroses, celandines and gravestones on a seat by the west door. Like most Catholic churches, however, the building itself is often locked.

Next, wander westward for 2 km, past both Ridlington and Westerland Farms, both tidy but unremarkable, through their fields and over their ditches, until you come to Lavington woods at Lower Barn, where you should turn right at the fingerpost. A dog may bark ineffectually at you at the last cottage, before you come to the felled pine woods of Lavington Common. The National Trust is here reclaiming the common back to a very pleasant open heath. You cross all of this in a north-easterly direction, ignoring three yellow arrows trying to take you left, right, left – in that order. This is not an easy walk to navigate, so you've done pretty well: I was helped by the view of a pure white Morris far ahead shining like a little beacon among the pine trees.

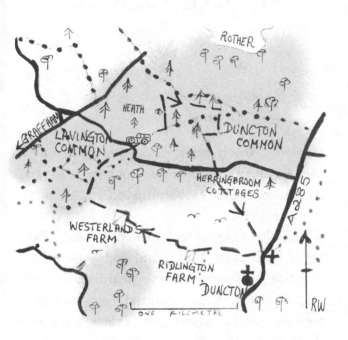

ROTHER

GRAFFHAM

LAVINGTON COMMON

HEATH

DUNCTON COMMON

HERRINGBROOM COTTAGES

A 285

WESTERLANDS FARM

RIDLINGTON FARM

DUNCTON

ONE KILOMETRE

RW

Lord's Piece

Here is a lovely walk of 5.3 km (3.25 miles)
over heath, wood, meadow, country lanes and
streams across the **Barlavington Estate** south
of Fittleworth.

You'll find a big car park roadside at Lord's Piece
between **Burton Mill pond** and **Watersfield**
(SU992169). The interpretive board at the gate
leads into magnificent heathland, being reclaimed
for rare insects such as field crickets and silver-
studded blue butterflies. The open-access land has
many paths, but from the pond walk north-east
up the side of valley – note masses of bell heather,
ling and tormentil flowers hereabouts. The
lovely escarpment of **Bignor** and **Bury Hills**

will appear to the right, where white birch trees contrast with orange of autumn bracken.

Near the house just before the road, and just before you leave Lord's Piece, note a wide but flattened tumulus which is about 3,500 years old. Take the bridle gate out to lane and turn half right at the blue arrow, which descends past a cone-prolific pine. After 350 m turn left at the fingerpost, down a sandy ravine on the Serpent Trail. Take the next left at the blue arrow, under overhead cables. There's a good tree-trunk seat here, at which you can contemplate the woodpeckers' handiwork on the birch in front.

Keeping left, with the cables overhead to your left, find a footbridge and the path ahead along an avenue of oaks. As you pass the meadow on the left, note the tiniest pond to your right, where I have watched a rare grey wagtail bathing. Pass by Triphill Farm and onto the busy and dangerous road; turn right and very soon left, leaving the road opposite Woodleigh House, to find a path across the meadow. Enter Waltham Park woods and a path that wanders south-east for about 800 m. You will pass dense, tall Norway spruce plantations after the oak and hazel coppice and the flash stream. Watch out for a fingerpost pointing right, but it is 10 m ahead of the actual turning. Note a pretty crop of birch trees, then a stand of red oaks – observe their huge leaves: could they be *Quercus x hispanica 'Lucombeana'*, I've often wondered. The Lucombe oak was first reared in 1762 in Devon, I believe. An oak is not necessarily just an oak!

At the road turn right, through more shady oaks leading to the main road. Cross this to a wide grass verge, then turn right and walk for 100 m, turning left into Horncroft Farm lane. Pass the famous Coates Common nature reserve to left (wet meadowland with rare plants and insects can be found here) and keep straight on past the house into heath woodland with holly trees.

Traverse the steep sandy gully and go on over the footbridge, to rejoin your old path. Walk uphill, then left, keeping 'pig town' to your left, then, 80 m after a nine-stemmed oak, go through the gate back into Lord's Piece. Take the route between four tall Corsican pines heading south-west and over the hill. From this point I can see the Morris far below, like an old white cow waiting for someone to take her home.

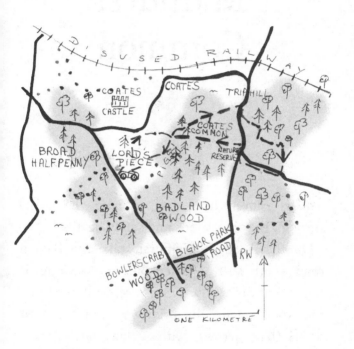

ONE KILOMETRE

35

Midhurst
Common

This is a lovely little stroll of 3 km (1.8 miles) through the pine woods and sandy heaths.

On the A286 in Midhurst, take the Bepton road south-west – after 300 m, parking is possible at SU877209. From here, walk west into the woods along the bridleway and **Serpent Trail** (blue arrow), with willow, birch, Scots pine, honeysuckle and old dead oaks covered by brambles. The old sandpit, out of sight to the right, was once the source of material for the famous Midhurst Whites bricks. Varying degrees of water here sometimes attract an unusual bird or two, such as a common sandpiper.

Note one patch of very beautiful grass in a glade on the right: this is wavy hair grass. The droopy flower stalks at the top of this grass are slightly wavy and the florets shine silvery in the sun. Turn right at the blue arrow marker to cross the route of an ancient railway line where a bridge once stood. After curving right, follow the route below an overhead power cable for about 700 m north-east. The Severals pines are on the left; ahead you'll see a recently cleared area suitable for nightjars to nest in. Make sure your dog is on its lead if walking during the summer breeding season. Note the bilberry, young ling and also bell heather and cross-leaved heather starting to grow again after the scrub clearance, with tufts of purple moor grass as well: an excellent bit of habitat management. There is even a small area of bog with pond skaters, as black as Guinness but not so tasty.

All around you'll see the reddish-bronze trunks of the Scots pines, rising like cathedral organ pipes and giving an ethereal air to this pleasant place. Crossing under the overhead power cables, at the large double pole number twenty-three, veer right on the yellow arrow route through rhododendrons, seeing how they kill all other vegetation. Walk up a slight hill and then down, finding a yellow arrow route to your right.

Keep ahead on the yellow arrows (three) to arrive at a small house, where you should turn left along the track curving to the right, eventually coming to an old cemetery. There is also a play area with swings and skateboard ramps here, and a bigger car park that could be used for this walk. Cowdray Estate has erected an information board here telling you that among the rare plants on the common are marsh violet, hare's-tail cottongrass and round-leaved sundew. Continue south past this notice and on past a wild playground, coming eventually to the road where you should take a sharp left, then a sharp right onto the main road. Note the ancient railway bridge walls here, between which the road runs, back to the beginning where I see the Morris, as white as those Midhurst Whites and just as nice to handle.

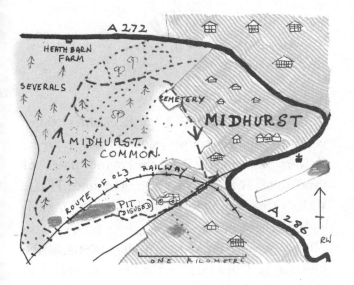

Queen's Corner

This Wealden walk of 4 km (2.5 miles) takes you into timeless countryside of ancient trees, flowery meadows, little hills and dales of sandstone. It has hardly changed since H. G. Wells's time and before him Benjamin Disraeli walked these lanes.

There is very limited roadside parking at the junction to Tentworth on the Stedham–Milland road at SU852243. From here, head north into a hollow, holly tree tunnel known as **Sharver's Lane** (this might become a stream in wet weather). All these rues have been embanked at some time past with sandstone walls. Chestnut coppice shows England's ancient industry when, until the 1950s, these woods produced hurdles, wheel spokes, charcoal, firewood and even kitchen utensils, to name but a fraction of the objects made from the raw material here, which is now no longer wanted.

At Stubb's Farm, the path kinks right then left near some old Lawson's cypresses and wanders into a rough meadow of wild grasses such as heath-bent. Why are there so many pits, banks and hollows in this place, I have wondered. The pits to the left resemble old carp ponds as found near monasteries, but they are now dried up. The path passes a corner of wire fence, near an old silver birch and an oak, and follows the fence north to a stile and ancient fingerpost that points into the woods, which takes you between a holly and a mammoth beech, and down along a broken wall that looks almost Roman.

Here you are on Dunner Hill – 'dunner', in Old English, simply means 'hill'. Hollies and hazel here lean all over the place, released into eccentric shapes. Another mighty oak watches over yet another rustic stile, after which the route dives down and left into Queen's Corner. Which queen was this, you might ask? Keep left, walking along the hedge, but soon look for a right turn through a little gate, into a garden and out the other side. The path kinks left and then right back into woods to Titty Hill. Here, keep to the right-hand side and go past the green, staying on the hard track southward to Bowley Farm. You'll see willows in a swamp, then a climb and finally a lovely view of the downland ridge ahead. Passing the farm, go through an iron gate into a big meadow, keeping to the big holly hedge on your left, before entering Oakham Common Wood. The oaks here have splendid epicormic growths, and there are also some big Scots pines.

Reaching Tentworth House, with its ornamental trees (red oaks, acacias, yews, spindles) keep on and walk to the right through the grounds, turning right (west) into the road and back to the start, where I find the ornamental old Morris with its ash-wood coachwork and tin of humbugs.

Racton Monument

Here is a chance to see the famous Racton Monument and enjoy 6.3 km (3.9 miles) of meadows, woods, lanes and views near the Ems Valley near the Hampshire border.

A car park can be found at **Walderton** (SU787104) at the junction with B2146, the Emsworth to West Marden road. Go north-east on the main road for 200 m, branching left into Woodlands Lane and uphill past cottages and under small beech trees. **Lordington Copse** will appear on your left as you reach the top of the hill where you should bear left into an ancient Sussex 'shaw', or safe wide track, through what was once difficult terrain. Ash, oaks, hazel, beech and wild apple trees make a pleasant avenue.

After 2 km you will come to the edge of **Stansted Park**. Turn left onto the yellow arrow route, through open woods where new oaks have been planted, then walk right and arrive at an open cornfield ahead. A notice here asks you to keep to the line of the path across these fields – not all that easy because the fingerposts either side of this field are not aligned. Look out for **Stansted House**, which will come into view on the right. Millions of flints in this field make it look like an ancient paved square gone to ruin, and tree clumps and avenues make this a Romantic landscape. Crossing the second field hopefully brings you to the opposite arrow and a hollow, holding one large horse chestnut and three sweet chestnut trees. At the cottage and barking spaniel turn sharply to the left into **Park Lane**.

Note the elm suckers and butcher's broom, which in winter have masses of red berries, and field maples down this ancient rue. There are also turkey oaks, useless as timber but beloved of old landscape planners. The lane then dips into a boggy hollow, causewayed for the carriages of centuries past. You'll see an underground reservoir to your left, with **Racton Monument** to your right. The monument was built in 1770 as a folly: today it lies in ruins and is all the more Romantic for it.

Here also are wonderful views of Chichester Harbour and Cathedral. Racton church, which can be seen below in the **River Ems** valley, has been much restored but its original thirteenth-century bits are visible, such as a showy canopied tomb like that in Boxgrove. The lane ends at a road junction where you should turn left. The usually dry stream bed makes a rough walkway off the road: but in only 200 m you should walk left by rails into a meadow with horses. Unused stiles show the way to the drive into **Lordington House** – here take the path and pass along the valley, keeping the reed grass to your right. You may encounter more inquisitive horses and two unusually tall alder trees in the valley to the right. The next field you'll come to is arable land, which you should cross uphill diagonally, keeping the distant cottages to your right and the woods to your left. Enjoy the lovely views of Bow Hill yew and beech woods high to the right. Reaching the road, eventually, turn right to the start point, where I find the Morris, an old Romantic ruin in the classical style.

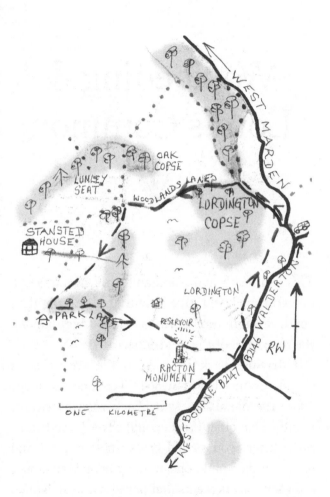

Woolbeding &
Lord's Common

This is a heath and woodland walk of 6 km (3.8 miles) around the **King Edward VII Hospital**, north of Midhurst, which is perched high among the pine trees of the sandstone.

If driving, park roadside in the West Sussex County Council bay at SU864254 on Liphook Road. Cross the dangerous switchback road eastward, uphill into a quiet bracken and silver birch heath. Soon after, you should cross another road and onto a sunken path, one of many hereabouts, once built for convalescents and paved with sandstone. Cross the muddy track and keep on ahead on the yellow arrow route and the New Lipchis Way. At the tidy little farm, turn left, still on the yellow route, into a gully where a female yew clasps the crag, then right at the yellow arrow marker, where squirrels forage sweet chestnuts. The Downs should be visible to the right.

Pass under the overhead power cables along a path that wanders a bit, but do not turn right on the obvious vehicle track: keep on ahead. Note the remnants of heather and purple moor grass, with its stiff stems, most of which has been destroyed by the bracken. Next the path starts to climb north-east through gorse – this is where you could see a wintering Dartford warbler, and nightjars in summer.

Reaching a minor road, where there is another car park, turn right and follow for about 1 km. You will see an enormous beech next to you on the right with a girth roughly 6 m (20 ft) or so. There are also silver birches, pines and sweet chestnuts. At this point you should be near the back of the hospital. Turn left onto the main road and, after 350 m, having walked past some young chestnut coppice, you should come to a cottage on your right, just before which is a footpath sign. Take the straight-ahead, level path south-south-west through the woods and keep to the yellow arrow route if you find it.

Eventually, after 500 m, you'll arrive at some cross-paths. Turn right along a stone-made path, following a sandstone wall. The path veers left among holly bushes and drifts of chestnut leaves, in front of the hospital that should here be half-hidden behind trees. Pass two strange old trees: chestnuts to the right, and beech to the left, which has an old woodpecker's hole. Head over the causeway and eventually cross a stile back into **Woolbeding Common**, where, again, you can view the Downs in all their glory if you look to your left.

Here an old wooden seat allows for contemplation. Next, turn right on the yellow arrow route uphill, and note the area being grazed by old breeds of cattle with which the National Trust are reclaiming the flowers and rare grasses. After 1 km turn left back onto the original path, with a fine view to the north. Retrace your steps downhill, being very careful as you cross the main road – comparatively speaking, modern cars are silent, swift and deadly and give no warning of their approach. The Morris you can hear.

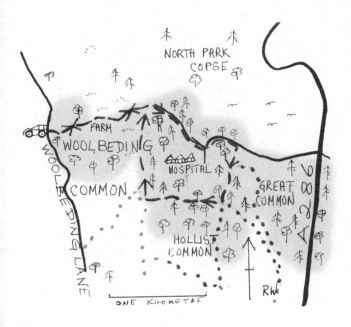

NORTH PARK COPSE

FARM

WOOLBEDING

WOOLBEDING LANE

COMMON

HOSPITAL

GREAT COMMON

HOLLIST COMMON

RW

ONE KILOMETRE

Country Park
& Estate
Walks

Angmering
Park Estate

A walk of 6.7 km (4.2 miles) through wonderful woodlands 2 miles east of Arundel.

Parking bays can be found on the sharp bend in the minor road north-east of Warningcamp village at TQ046074. Take bridle road north, past the big red welcome sign, into the fields between hedges, with wild roses, blackberries, old man's beard, and views to Arundel and beyond. You may see whitethroat warblers in spring and summer, and skylarks all year round here.

The track bends right and downhill, where there's a hidden quarry to your right and good chalk turf banks with bird's foot trefoil. A steep valley lies to the left with cattle-grazing downland, where a steep track stretches down over slippery chalk. At the bottom of the hill, go straight ahead at the blue arrow for about 90 m, then right at the fingerpost, past another red sign for about 30 m, then right again onto Monarch's Way, and uphill into the woods. Here you can spot masses of dog's mercury, with tiddly holes in the leaves eaten by dog's mercury beetles. Wayside plants also include yellow archangel and woundwort.

At the top of the slippery hill go straight on at the fingerpost crossways, continue on Monarch's Way, and you'll soon come to a five-track crossway where new fingerposts have been put up. Stay on Monarch's Way, which is the metalled road straight ahead through the well-managed beech plantation. The trees here are well-spaced, I suppose about sixty years old. Listen for blackcap warblers singing; in spring masses of bluebells appear throughout this walk. Carry on for about 1 km where you'll come to an open meadow on your left. Also, one can find wild strawberries on the roadside bank here.

Next, turn left next, keeping the meadow to your left and the nice pine wood to your right, leaving the smooth road. The path follows the edge of a wheat field, passing Upper Barpham Farm with its Shetland ponies and donkeys, climbing up to reveal a noble view of the downland ahead. Here you can have lunch and drink in the views, as they say, as well as perhaps some orange juice. Next, turn sharply left into the meadow, keeping the trig point far to your right as you cross the col to find a blue arrow route which takes a sharp left along a lovely cranky old hedge of misshapen oaks and hawthorns. New views of Houghton Chalk Quarry, Bignor Hill and Arundel Castle can be enjoyed here.

After passing another red welcome sign, cross the vehicle track made of bits of old concrete block and dive into the woods, which in spring will be fragrant with bluebells. Note many old deep pits along the way, from which stone was quarried to build the track you are on for the next 2 km. Here you'll spot lovely old beech trees on the 'shaw' banks through these hazel woods. Notice how Angmering Park Estate has sensibly left the remains of the old trees be.

You will arrive back onto the metalled road and should follow it south-west, crossing Monarch's Way, downhill to start – for me back to the old Morris with its red seats of welcome.

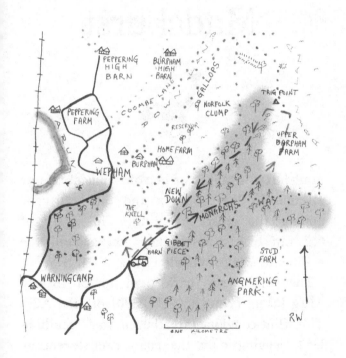

Dale Park, Madehurst

Madehurst is said to be one of the most remote villages in West Sussex and the landscape among the most charming. This walk of 6.2 km (3.7 miles) takes you around the eighteenth-century Dale Park.

There is a car park next to **St Mary Magdalen church** (SU985100) off the A29. This flint-conglomerate church was rebuilt in 1864, leaving only the plain twelfth-century west door. Look through a window (the church is kept locked) to see a remarkable red marble font. The Burne-Jones stained glass windows were blown out by a V1 Doodlebug in 1944. Observe the male yew to the east and female to the west, both suffering strange dieback. Grand gravestones reveal there was once a rich past, now diminished, with fewer people in area nowadays than in recorded history.

Set off north on the road, bend left, downhill, and left again onto the yellow arrow route, along a smooth farm road. Ahead, cedars show where Dale Park used to be. At New Barn Farm, continue over the footpath crossways to climb a hill, curving right. Be sure to stop and admire the boxwood growing everywhere – a favourite pheasant cover of Victorian gamekeepers. This whole estate appears to have been devoted to game shooting and gracious landscaping combined. Next, go left on the yellow arrow route near the kennels and square flint house, and keep walking west-south-west. Soon you will join a granite gravel track – note the World War Two Nissen huts hidden in the woods. After emerging into the open you can view Glatting Beacon on Bignor Hill to the right.

Stay on the track bending left downhill, then turn sharply right into the downland meadows. Follow the tractor-wheel marks down into a fine valley and walk up the other side. Here, note the ancient metal fencing around the park coverts. Turn sharply left and walk between two old beech trees, one of which has been shot at with a 12-bore shotgun. Climb over the stile, sticking to the yellow arrow route, and follow the path south-south-east through a serviceable beech plantation, which, unfortunately, has been damaged by grey squirrels. Leave the wood but follow the grass causeway into the valley. At a cattle pen, take a sharp right uphill into the woodland, curving left, following the wood's edge right down to Chichester Lodge. Here, turn sharply to the left onto a smooth track. The new Dale Park House can be seen far up to your left. The old house, built in 1784, was pulled down in 1959.

Near the A29, pass under another old cedar, then turn right, and climb over a stile onto the yellow arrow route. Follow the wood's edge north-east and, at the next track, take the kink left, then go right at the stile onto a tractor track through a cereal field. Fairmile Bottom is on your right. Pass through a brief woodland to arrive on what looks like an old gallops with an avenue of ash trees. Southern Water reservoirs

are under your feet; at their pumping station
turn right, back onto the recent path. Walk
uphill to the church: where I return to the old
Morris, white as the gravestones there.

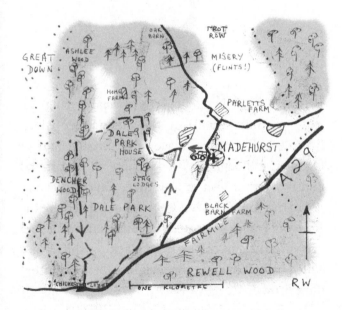

Petworth Park

Petworth Park is particularly special during the 'rut' (mating period) of the fallow deer which live there. This takes place in the second half of October, although the herd is there all year round and is worth a visit at any time. Fallow deer are not native to Britain but were imported here by the Romans from the eastern Mediterranean. There are variations in colour from black to white (once called white harts), the original being spotted dark brown.

Parking is available roadside at SU973214, where you enter the park by the southern lodge gate. As this is the perfect place to simply wander around I will not give a particular walk distance, except to say that I usually cover about 3 km (2 miles) to see the best of it. Cross the football field, which is often covered during the old goose fair time with a sheen of silken gossamer from millions of tiny spider parachutes – this is the autumn spiders' 'festival'. There are many internal footpaths through the park: it is best to keep to them so as not to disturb the deer too much. Notices ask you not to remove anything from the park e.g. conkers, deer antlers, fungi, etc. as these all provide the deer with special mineral traces.

After the field you will come to the upper pond, part of the Capability Brown landscaping of 1752, and also known as the Serpentine Lake, where waterbirds including Canada geese, kingfishers, great crested grebes, moorhens, coots, grey and pied wagtails, wood ducks and gadwalls reside.

In 1770 the Duchess of Northumberland, while visiting the park, described the clumps of chestnuts, oaks and beeches as being of 'stupendous size and surpassing all that I have seen in my life'. Many are still there and have now been reinforced with new specimens. I usually walk north-west along the hard track, crossing the deer park hill where one can enjoy spectacular views of the great deer herd. At the time of the rut the older and stronger bucks with the biggest set of antlers (known as 'stand bucks', as they defend a particular 'stand' to hold their harem of does) clash in spectacular fighting as they try to keep competitors at bay. The bucks collect plant debris in their palmate antlers to enhance their appearance, groaning deeply to show off to rivals and keep the does interested; the does bleat in excitement. There is much chasing off of younger bucks and chasing after errant does; the scene seethes with noise and movement. Eventually, the stand buck becomes exhausted and moves aside for a rest, thus giving competitors the opportunity they have eagerly awaited.

When you have feasted enough on this annual spectacle, turn east towards the lower pond to look for birds. Return south-east to pass the upper pond along its eastern shore, noting the third Earl's boathouse and the bas-relief Neptune between its two arches, which is even earlier. There is a sense of wilderness and open space in the park which, with the large herds of animals visible all around in natural surroundings, gives a unique feeling of well-being, which I find enhanced by Morris waiting with a heart as white as any hart.

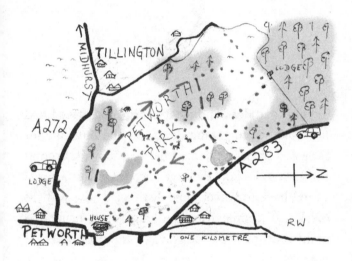

Stansted Park

Trying to understand what a large dog otter I had heard about might be doing on the outskirts of Stansted Park last year, I decided to walk around the area to look at the sort of country this animal would have to travel. The distance of the walk is 6.7 km (4.3 miles) for the long route, using the main road part of the way, or 5 km (3 miles) if not.

Parking can be found in Stansted's car park (SU754103), opposite the lodge gates, off the Westbourne–Forestside road. From here, cross the road out of the park and walk past the lodge, heading east into North Coopers Wood along the road. There is a magnificent beech tree and two turkey oaks to pass under. Once in the dip in the meadow, turn sharply right onto the blue arrow route, along the fence-line penning Jacob sheep. Cross the famous wide western sightline (avenue) to **Stansted House**. Passing by the garden centre entrance, keep right on the tarmac road, then turn left into the meadows indicated by the yellow arrow route. In the oak grove ignore the first stile on the left and walk straight ahead over the next stile – note fine heath bent grasses. To your far left you'll get a brief view of the Racton Monument.

Next follow the raised embankment, which was made 150 years ago for the purposes of a park drive, through a splendid avenue of giant redwoods and Californian redwoods (*Sequoia wellingtonia* and *S. sempervirens*). This becomes marshy ground with occasional winter streams; I can imagine an otter exploring this wood.

After passing a huge single pine, there is a stile – take **Park Lane**, which goes to the left, for the shorter, safer walk avoiding the main road. Join the main road for the longer walk, in order to see both **Brickkiln Ponds**, but beware as the road is dangerous. It's easy to imagine an otter on the ponds here, catching roach, bream, tench and possibly a moorhen or two. Turn left off the road, after the old watercress beds, to Sindles Farm, finally meeting Park Lane and crossing it to a grove of oaks, sweet chestnuts and one horse chestnut tree. Follow the nearest yellow arrow to cross a kale field north-east. Soon you'll pass just left of some ancient lime trees, with a back view of Stansted House. Cross the eastern sightline of young beech, planted in memory of the ninth Earl, after passing two beech clumps and aim for the farthest gap in the hedge ahead. Here turn left onto Monarch's Way, with a view of the Isle of Wight to your left. This track joins the road back at the start, where I return to the Morris, which in its day carried a road casualty otter found dead on Devon roads.

For those interested to know more, Stansted's tempestuous history is best explained in the Earl of Bessborough's book *Enchanted Forest – the Story of Stansted in Sussex* (Weidenfeld & Nicholson, 1984), detailing the Civil War and Charles II, with ancestral portraits, eighteenth-century gravures of the estate, the chapel made famous by Keats' poem 'The Eve of St Agnes', and the fire of 1900, among many more events in its chequered past. The house itself is well worth a visit.

Watergate Park, Walderton

This is West Sussex at its best: a lovely walk of 6.4 km (4 miles) through woods, fields, gentle slopes and with glimpses of the sea.

Park at the roadside at SU787105, just west of **Walderton** village next to the winterbourne River Ems, which drains the Stoughton valley. Set off north up the B2147, past Cooks Lane, then turn right onto the blue arrow route between the dual hedgerows. An extraordinary display of hawthorn berries can be seen here in autumn, with almost tame blackbirds feasting. Note all the ivy flowers, too, feeding red admirals and wild bees in the autumn sun.

Next turn right onto the road for 200 m uphill, then left on the yellow arrow route into some cereal fields. On your right, the edges of the massive yew forest at Kingley Vale appear, with 1950s beech plantations on Bow Hill, which rises to 260 m. At the end of this field is a seat, a useful place to stop for a rest or to have lunch; observe the spindle bush next to it with its pink seed cases, also the blackthorn with sloes. Then keep going north-east to a woodland where another, better seat, this time with a terrific view of the silver Solent to the south-east, can be found. Turn sharply left downhill, through woods with silver birch, hazel, dogwood and some older, biggish beech that survived the hurricane of October 1987, and which have unusually large seed husks. Your path will show the marks of the cleaves of fallow deer, which use this way at night. Cross the road at the bottom of the path into an area with oak and hazel – this has the strange name of **Piglegged Row Wood**, where butcher's broom and the unusual grass wood mellick shows in brownish patches everywhere. After 250 m turn left onto the blue arrow route to follow the edge of the woods. Splendid chalk grassland banks are found here, rich with marjoram in summer, and orchids and butterflies including brown argus. The path eventually turns right at the blue arrow route marker, into Woodbarn Wood, and soon you'll find a left turn into Watergate Park.

I have noted the ash trees dying here and wondered why. Also, why has the old railed, but dry, pond here not been reinstated? Follow the old iron railing down to Waterbeach House. This was a grand affair, rebuilt by Sir John Soane in around 1790, and again in 1882, demolished in the past century, but apparently now rebuilt yet again in the classic Parthenon style. Some specimens of beech and Corsican pines can be seen here.

Cross the road at Lodge House into Watergate Hanger. Then turn left around the back of shady houses to follow this lovely woodland path south. Meet Monarch's Way again, left, trickling downhill back to the beginning: where I find the old Morris chatting to 'moderns' by the Ems.

Labels on map: HASLETT COPSE, BUSTO COPSE, FARM, INHOLMES WOOD, WATERGATE HANGER, WATERGATE PARK, PIGLEGGED ROW, LORDINGTON COPSE, WALDERTON, ONE KILOMETRE, R.W.

Downland
Walks

Beacon Hill

This is a downland walk of 5.3 km (3.4 miles), with spectacular views and a visit to a Bronze Age hill fort.

  Parking can be found under the beech trees on the west side of the B2141 Chilgrove–South Harting road at SU796173. From here, cross the road east into Kill Devil Copse, which lies on the blue arrow route alongside a meadow. A new metal gate on your right allows access into Telegraph House and a great yew forest, also with large old hazel trees. At the meadow's end turn sharply left, downhill, with a mighty beech tree and steep slope below. Soon you'll arrive at the junction of Whitcombe and

Bramshott Bottom, with a small re-made dewpond in view. This area always reminds me of the kind of historic meeting place chosen by Thomas Hardy for the enactment of a dramatic moment in a novel.

Next, follow the yellow arrow route ahead into Bramshott Bottom. In winter this is a lonely, rather eerie place with desert colours from dry grasses. I once saw a pair of stonechats here. The hawthorn and yew scrub high to the left and to the right holds many woodland birds. This valley, scoured by the ancient Ice Age, climbs eventually to its end on the chalk ridge between Harting Down to the left and Beacon Hill to the right.

From here, turn right to climb the steep steps onto Beacon Hill, which is 242 m (794 ft) high. Note a juniper bush near a small ash tree, and fine downland turf over the whole of this sheep and deer-grazed nature reserve. Views at the top are described on a National Trust orienteering plinth, although for some unknown reason they have left out Steep Hill above Petersfield. Nonetheless, there are brilliant views of the steep downland escarpment both to the east and the west. Here the Neolithic and Bronze Age hill-fort banks are intact but the land at their centres has been cultivated.

Continue east near the trees until you reach a steep hill running downwards, as West Dean Estate's **Millpond Bottom** appears below you to the right. Note the ancient, triple-defensive bank ahead. Next, turn sharply right at the cross-tracks onto the **South Downs Way**, southwards, passing Murray Downland Trust's **Under Beacon Nature Reserve** on left. Approaching the woodland, turn sharply right, staying on the SDW for 500 m, then take the sharp left into the gorse scrub, downhill back to the two bottoms, looking for the lovely ant castles and yellow hill ants that live in them.

Cross your earlier path through the small metal gate, passing a yew tree layering its branches to form new trees, then head uphill on a path curving right, to again pass Kill Devil Copse meadow, on your left. On reaching the main road, follow the woodland path next to it on the left, downhill and back to the start. Here I see the old Morris gleaming as white as the Beacon Hill fort chalk and the ossuary of its ancient dramas. Who knows what happened there 3,000 years ago...

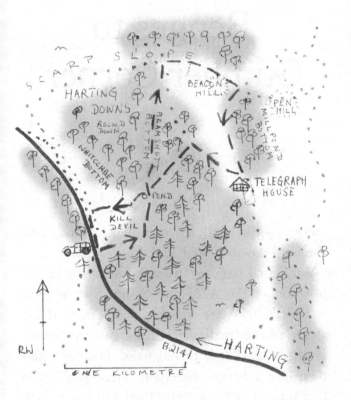

Benges to Gumber Corner

Here is a fine walk through beech woods and the high downs near Eartham Woods.

You'll find parking in the large lay-by at the junction of the A285 and Selhurst Park road at SU939120. After crossing the main road (be aware of the traffic here) head eastwards past **Benges Cottage**, through the shrubbery and then into a beech plantation. Here you'll also find snakeskin maples with their brilliant yellow autumn leaves, put here half a century ago by the Forestry Commission, mixed with the lovely crop of beech: tall and well-managed. Drifts of

80

orange leaves lie along the wet track which heads north-east. Masses of flints can be found here – every one is 70 million years old and used to be high above where you walk today. As the track turns east at huge puddles, note the 3,000-year-old earthworks crossing the track, part of a vast complex of defensive barriers fortifying Sutton Down and Bignor Hill.

Pass two 200-year-old beech trees into open downland – this is a perfectly lovely little downland way, giving the feeling you could be deep inside another century. It is quiet here, the plain below fading into a silver sea. In the spring gorse is in bloom; you may find the scent of foxes in your nose and downland plants like fleabane and sheep's-bit at your feet.

Far ahead what look like smooth-wave clouds become the blue curve of the down slopes of **Amberley Mount.** The narrow strip of woodland to the left is a remnant of a 600-year-old hazel coppice, used for centuries to make sheep hurdles. Shrubs I have noted here include wayfaring, dogwood, blackthorn and spindle. Soon the woodland strip is on your right, where lots of robins and wrens hide. At the crossways turn left on the blue arrow route, joining **Stane**

Street and also Monarch's Way. The Romans raised this road with embankment. Look for a polypody fern growing out of an ash tree. Cross another 3,000-year-old earthwork and, soon after, turn sharply left back onto the South Downs Way, re-crossing that earthwork. A little further and you'll enter the sheep-grazed National Trust downland – the view to the left is one of the best in Britain, with the Isle of Wight and the coastal plain visible.

Reaching a five crossways, take the second left at the new fingerpost, with a little wood of hazel and yew to left – look out for a fallow deer harbour (resting place) here. Soon join the outward track, which you will follow back to the start.

I wonder if you will spot the tumulus on your right in the beech wood, 400 m after the puddles? Or you may be lucky enough, as I was, to meet the lady riding in the trap with the Morris Minor wheels, pulled by the old white mare. More charming even than my old white Morris and even cheaper to run – well, trot. Which of us has the higher horsepower, though?

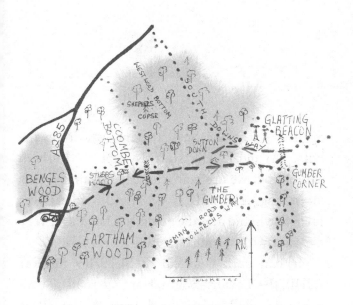

Bevis's Thumb

Sir Bevis was the Sussex giant, who rode the horse Arundel. His staff is kept in Bosham church, but we are going to see his thumb – it is 90 m long. The walk is 4.5 km (2.8 miles) over farm downland and the going is firm: it's all very pleasant with splendid views.

You can park your car at SU797169 just off B2141, the Lavant–South Harting road. There is a leafy bay beneath beech trees on the left as you're heading north-west to the top of the hill, opposite Kill Devil Copse. Walk south-west, noting the extraordinary, grandiose Parthenon arch above the wrought iron gates, all attached to a normal brick house in the woods. What can it mean? I must find out. The bridlepath kinks to the left, to follow the trees, and then splits by a thick blackthorn bush. Take a right turn onto the blue arrow route to follow power lines along the left edge of a mini gallops, which is itself an interesting strip of ancient downland turf. Views to the left are of the back of Kingley Vale and at times the two famous Bronze Age bell barrows are visible on skyline 6.5 km (4 miles) south-east. Half right is Jubilee Clump on Chalton Down hilltop, farther right is Windmill Hill (8 km/5 miles).

Soon **Uppark** appears on your right, just over a mile north-west. At the end of the gallops, veer right through a metal gate and into a field. When I did this walk in winter I found an old bullfinch's nest thirty-four paces on at eye height, on the left in the blackthorn, which still had a tiny fragment of blue eggshell in it. It is worth looking to see what is there when you do this walk. Next follow the rue of beeches – observe the mole plough left to rust here, an antique now. Notices here say 'Cattle please shut gate'. I hope the cows can read! After reaching the minor road, cross over it to find the Neolithic long barrow running to the left along the edge of the road, also known as Bevis's Thumb (you may find salad burnet growing on it). But if this was his thumb, what a monstrous knight he was! He was, of course, able to wade across to the Isle of Wight.

Continue east along the road, passing gardens with guinea fowl and hens, climbing the hill to find a pleasant stile upon which to sit beneath the power cable. I once saw several stonechats here, perching on a wire. Walk onwards to find the road junction to Up Marden. Here, turn left over the stile to follow the rue due north along the edge of some fields. You will find hazel, hawthorn, holly, Scots pine, whitebeam, ash and oak in this area, which is called the Edgar Plantation.

A 3,500-year-old small tumulus lies at the end, almost forgotten and covered with trees, especially two old ash. Soon you join your original path and follow this back. For me, the Morris awaits, as white as the snowdrops near the Parthenon arch.

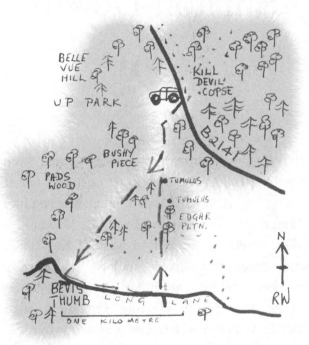

Buriton Downs

The Sussex South Downs Way runs from Beachy Head to Buriton, so let us have a closer look at **Buriton** itself, even though it is just into Hampshire. This downland walk of 3.8 km (2.4 miles) starts by the village pond at SU739200, where eighty assorted mallard and twelve moorhens will be grateful for a bit of bread.

Take the South Harting–Petersfield road (B2141), and turn off left onto the Buriton byroad, running on to the A3. **St Mary's Church**, by the spring pond, is well worth a look, with its sombre interior, intricate windows, twelfth-century Purbeck marble font, thirteenth-century wall paintings in the three rare *sedilia* with stepped arches, and the In memoriam World War One wall tablets to Bonham Carters, one of whom was killed aged forty-seven on the first day of the Battle of the Somme. Note the female Irish and Atlantic yews in the churchyard, also the unusual sawara cypress. Walk to the far edge of the pond into South Lane, past clunch-chalk cottages with thatched roofs, and under a nice old railway bridge with brick dovetailing, which carries the main London line. Trains sound air horns here before this imminent tunnel and pedestrian crossing. Huge beech trees and a lime said to be 1,000 years old can be seen here, as well as lovely hart's-tongue ferns on the steep damp banks. There is a bird reserve to your left as you climb the oncoming slope, curving left all the way. Woodpeckers, nuthatches, marsh tits and owls dwell in this ancient chalk pit. Halls Hill FC car park is at the top of the rise.

Turn sharply left to follow the little woodland path next to the road as you walk south-east. The precipice on your left, sensibly fenced, shows white sludge of a possible spring far below. The road is part of the South Downs Way, so join it to remain on top of the Downs. Next you will pass a nearby underground reservoir – the view to the left is supreme; one can see all the way into Surrey. In the hedgerows in the autumn, notice the masses of red berries growing on black bryony plants (*Tamus communis*), the best I have ever seen. The view behind is of Queen Elizabeth Country Park. Pass under some 'Eiffel Tower' power cables down into a dip to **Coulters Dean**, then follow the road left past the Hampshire & Isle of Wight Wildlife Trust nature reserve sign. Turn left again here, by two ancient damaged beech trees, to walk downhill, westward. Buzzards hang-glide this slope in northerlies. This track is called the **Milky Way** – here you'll see various woodland orchids in the summer. At the bottom the track switches right then, at its muddiest point 100 m later, look for a stile taking you left into some meadows.

Find three or four more stiles leading through cattle or sheep-grazing land back to the beginning, where I see Milky Way Morris communing with mallards.

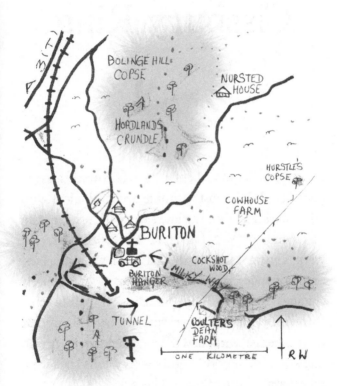

91

Cissbury Ring

Here is a brilliant walk of 4.2 km (2.5 miles) around one of the UK's most stunning archaeological sites.

For parking, find the large car park off the A24, just north of **Worthing** at TQ129077. Take the white arrow route north-east, past white poplars, onto a wooded pathway where the arrow properly changes to blue. Some remains of old beeches thrown by the 1987 hurricane are here, as well as a rich hedge with hawthorn, blackthorn, privet, dogwood, sycamore, and huge ivy tods sheltering hibernating butterflies and bees.

Coming to a small woodland at some rusty gates, turn left on the blue arrow route, noting berberis and box, and a spindle, just before the gate into a meadow. Here you will see some fine old chalk grassland with scabious, hawkbits, salad burnet, and eight species of orchids in spring and summer.

This downland is centuries old and traditionally grazed by sheep to keep it short. A rarity over this hill is field fleawort, and twenty-eight species of butterfly have been recorded here, including the rare adonis blue. After following the wire fence you will arrive at another car park and information panel. Six paths cross here; take the second on the right, on the blue arrow route south-east. Keep the old, dry, dew pond to your right, as you go between two old hawthorns. Stop to observe the whitebeams and the edges of the great hill fort to the right. Hart's tongue ferns grow on a damp spring line here.

Climb for 450 m and then take the right fork to a swing gate. Go through the gate and turn sharply right, along the fence line and up to the huge ramparts of Cissbury Ring. Enter the precincts via another swing gate; you may have to watch out for a bull (harmless but do not antagonise), as old English longhorn cattle graze the 65 acres of this hill fort in an effort to keep down the scrub. All the cows have long horns, too, but those of the bull are longer than any. The best way to see this ancient city is to walk along the tops of its wall, taking the route left, south-west. The steep valley to the left is **Deep Bottom**, where the Romans had their vineyards. Note also, to your right, the straight banks which were Roman field boundaries. As the wall begins to bear right, take note of all the pits and hollows to the right, half-covered by scrub. These are the Neolithic flint mine shafts which go back 6,500 years. As the wall bends even further right, going north-east, look for concrete steps going left that take you off the rampart. Follow the path west, downhill over the meadows, back through **Hill Barn Covert** to the start. I find the old Morris asleep in her pen like an old Southdown sheep.

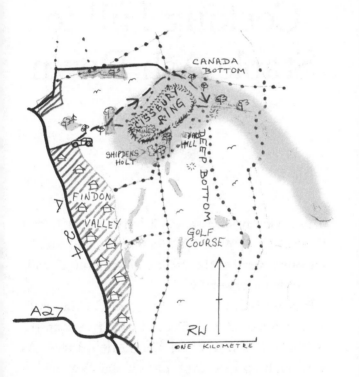

ONE KILOMETRE

Cocking Hill to Staple Ash Down

This is a lovely long walk of 10 km (6.2 miles) along the **South Downs Way** and downland woods, passing several of the chalk-ball 'sculptures' made by Andy Goldsworthy.

Parking is available at the top of Cocking Hill, on the A286, at SU875166. Start off west up the South Downs Way, along **Middlefield Lane**. As you climb up **Cocking Down** the view behind expands most wonderfully – you can see right over into Surrey. You will pass two steep valleys: **Stead Combe** to the right, **Warren Bottom** to the left. ('Bottom' is the more traditional Sussex name for a steep valley.) The bare fields at the top near the trig-point at 238 m on your right are a favourite haunt of skylarks, though these have declined alarmingly in the forty years that I have known this walk. Be sure to look out for the chalk balls as you walk.

Soon you will pass another small tumulus, this one to the left in a meadow. The South Downs Way then dips down and runs over some indistinct cross-dykes. After this you'll come to some water tanks where you should turn left, along a line of beech trees. Here you'll enter a spruce woodland – a good place to hear nightjars in summer, making their calls until late July. Stay south-south-west on this bridleway for 2 km, passing through **West Dean Woods**. Here it's important to keep dogs under tight control, as ground-nesting birds abound in the spring and summer, and there is pheasant shooting in the winter. In mid-March there is a magnificent spread of wild daffodils here and you will also see at least some of the 300 flowering plants in this reserve, not to speak of the forty species of birds and thirty species of butterflies, depending on the time of year. The track eventually passes through a meadow, emerging on the road above **Staple Ash Farm**.

At the road turn left, going uphill to the corner past one of chalk balls, where you should leave the road and go straight ahead to cross **Staple Ash Down**, then through the stile and down the rue, rejoining the road and keeping on straight ahead: here you are on a sharp S-bend, so be aware of fast cars. Turn the corner, then go left through the gate, turning north-east along the edge of the wood on your left, with fields on your right. Here you'll be on a cinder track made with cinders from Wales in about 1900 (to facilitate driving of carriages of the Royal shooting parties at West Dean). It's kite and skylark country right over **Colworth Down**. Soon you'll enter a mixed woodland used by the charcoal burners – stay north-east, keeping strictly to the yellow arrow route, to avoid wrongly taking any of the many woodland tracks. Then go left, and left again, to travel north-west between **Venus Wood** and **Stubbs Copse**. Listen for goldcrests and firecrests in the pines here. On reaching T-junction, turn right onto the yellow arrow route back north-east to rejoin the South Downs Way, going right, downhill, back to the start. I make my way to the Morris, solid as one of those chalk balls.

Duncton

This is a delightful walk of 4.5 km (2.7 miles) over the steep downs and past the water springs below them.

Parking is possible at the **Cricketers Inn**, on the A285 at SU960170, in Duncton. From here walk north-east along the pavement for 120 m, then turn right onto the blue arrow route past the South Downs Areas of Outstanding Natural Beauty notice. The track leads past a Local Heritage Initiative supported by nine agencies – from the RSPB to Natural England – which fund/approve this little coppice wood, with its tightly packed pole-like oak trees. Here, look out for the charcoal-burners' iron kiln. The road then bends right, where you will see primroses on its banks, and crosses Duncton Brook with its small colony of winter heliotrope. Huge horsetails grow in ditches here, as do clumps of pendulous sedge. Blue, great, marsh and long-tailed tits are seen commonly around this walk. Follow the track south past Duncton Mill fishery lake, then on past Barlavington Farm's buildings. The mill pond has shoals of trout, which will fascinate you as they continuously circle anti-clockwise. Note also the masses of mistletoe on all the poplar and derelict apple trees.

Head uphill past the mill and turn sharply left on the blue arrow route to climb into the rue, passing a heap of rusty rubbish. The rue passes an abandoned apple orchard with more mistletoe. Look out for a farm sign that says 'Drink in the view'; an advert for its organic herd. Marsh orchids and the rare lizard orchid appear somewhere here. Next, cross the road and continue up the steep hill, south-west on the blue arrow route, between the fences. Watch for 200-year-old pollarded ashes, all with nine stems, followed by two old beech trees. Here the path bends right; after reaching the two blue arrows, turn right and 80 m further on you'll find three more blue arrows; take the middle one. The track then crosses a very steep gulley. Ignore the last fingerpost before the main road and walk straight on along the track.

Next, cross the main road into the Viewpoint car park; here you can enjoy tremendous views across the Weald: far to the left is the Shoulder of Mutton hill beyond Petersfield at Steep. This was where the poet Edward Thomas lived until his departure, in 1917, for the battlefields and death three months later. To the right is Blackdown, home of the Victorian Poet Laureate, Alfred Lord Tennyson. For the Romans much of the Weald was a danger zone, due to bands of guerrilla fighters. Further back in time it was also a dangerous hunting ground for Stone and Bronze Age people harvesting wild animals, such as wolf and wild boar. Before that, prehistoric creatures roamed and seas foamed.

Walk west out of the car park, and turn sharply right downhill through yews, ash, whitebeams and badger diggings: you will find bluebells here in the spring. Turn left onto the fields, then cross the main road again. After 40 m take a sharp right along the edge of a garden, then soon left

along a hedge and a flint wall. Keep walking
straight ahead over the meadows to cross the
stream by the footbridge and up the other side to
turn right to the Cricketers Inn – where waits
the Morris all dressed in white as well.

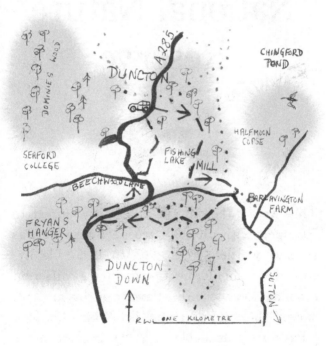

Kingley Vale
National Nature
Reserve

This walk takes in the finest yew forest in Europe, with 30,000 trees, where I was reserve warden from 1963 to 1995. Ideally, this walk should be taken during different seasons, to get the full flavour of this ancient, sacred place. The distance is 6.4 km (4 miles).

Parking is available at West Stoke, in the off-road County Council car park (SU825087), 250 m west of the church. From here, walk north, along the track and through the gate, for 1.2 km (0.75 miles). Bow Hill, which surrounds Kingley Vale, looms ahead – an outlier of the chalk downs. Soon you'll pass close to a Roman cesspit to your right, which has long been filled in. After the woods, there is a Bronze Age bank to the right which runs the length of next field. Once you've arrived at the gate to the nature reserve you'll see a small field centre ahead, built in 1965.

Continue north along the central valley path, passing three ancient pond declivities on the right, under the trees. Note the fallow deer high-browse line on all the trees around. In the spring, species of woodland birds singing here can number up to forty. Next, the path enters a woodland to the right, where you'll find the most ancient yew trees: about thirty of them, perhaps 2,000 years old, with girths of about 7 m. Look for the female yews with red berries, called arils: the red juice is edible but the pip is deadly poisonous. Emerge from the group of ancient trees into the valley centre and a vast natural amphitheatre will surround you: the steep slope ahead was carved by thaw springs during Ice Ages. Here also are dry ancient pond sites and downland meadows of flower-rich turf with 300 species. Observe the system of linear banks in the valley, marking fields of Bronze Age Roman farmers. A Romano/British village site is marked by pits and hollows. The slopes are covered by a young yew forest, only one or two centuries old.

Turn right (east), passing a modern dewpond (which I built in 1976, and was rebuilt in 2011), climb the eastern slope into the yews and continue on the left-handed circuit of the 1 km-wide dry valley, the site of a Viking battle in AD 859. There is evidence of Stone Age flint mines on the right (east) side of path near the top. Here, look right for the sarsen stone commemorating Sir Arthur Tansley, Britain's founder of nature conservation principles; this was his favourite view in Britain: out across the Chichester plain to the Isle of Wight, the Solent, Chichester Harbour, with Pagham Harbour to the south. On a clear summer's evening you can sometimes even see Beachy Head reflecting the setting sun; the view to the north reveals Hampshire and the South Downs, Uppark, and north-east to Monckton, the surrealist home of Edward James.

Walk on to pass four Bronze Age burial mounds, the 'Kings' Graves', which are 3,500 years old – two are bell barrows, two bowl. Keep left off the hill to complete the circular tour of valley. The yew wood on the steep hill below has 'family groups', showing how juniper bushes a century ago nursed yews against grazing animals. All the way down the hill in the summer there are wild orchids on its bank, plus many other flowers, and several of the thirty-five species of butterflies present on the reserve (as they appear throughout in their own season). Many breeding birds in the summer and migrants in the winter can be spotted (for example, redwings enjoying the yew berries).

The path then leads back to the reserve entrance where I survey Morris, looking like an old Bronze Age monument.

MONARCH'S WAY

DEVILS HUMPS

KINGLEY VALE

STOKE DOWN

WEST COPSE

STOKE WOODS

ONE KILOMETRE

WEST STOKE

RW

Lady Wood & Levin Down

Here is a lovely walk of 4.8 km (3 miles) over the **Goodwood Downs**.

Park at **Singleton Church** at SU878131. From the church, with its famous graffiti scratched on pillars in 1600 and the marble monument to Thomas Johnson of 1744, walk east along the village street to the modern school, turn left at the bus shelter and walk uphill, passing two huge western red cedars in the old graveyard.

The seat at the top here offers a view, from the left, of Charlton village, Goodwood grandstands, the Trundle Iron Age fort, West

Dean Arboretum, the Weald & Downland Open Air Museum, West Stoke clump, West Dean College, Bow Hill, Kingley Vale and Hat Hill: one couldn't ask for more!

Walk over the stile into a huge meadow with some quite good downland turf. Go right on the blue arrow route, near the old flint quarry, but soon bear left and look for a path going steeply down to the left. (The direction post was smashed when I walked this last.) Follow the woodland edge – more of an overgrown hedge, I suppose. Pass another broken sign along the fence and look out for a large holm oak. The turf here gets better and better; in season you will see common blue butterflies and harebells. Pass by an uprooted oak, then find a metal gate with a clasp, where you should bear left.

On reaching a stile, take the yellow arrow route into Collick's Copse, where ancient beeches and a curious unidentified earth bank, presumably Iron Age, can be found. Take the steep and slippery downhill through some brambles, with enchanter's nightshade growing by the way, to a gate with fleur-de-lis. Turn right, following the edge of Lady Wood to a house, then go right, along the road. You'll see a pretty valley of arable fields on the left, then a large meadow on the right, with meadow brown butterflies, red bartsia and goat's-beard. Note the owl box on an oak tree here. At the next house, turn right on the blue arrow route, and head straight up the hill along a sunken routeway, where the turf is rich with yellow hawkbits.

Next you will come to five crossways. Here you have a choice: you can either take the right-hand path, through an iron gate back onto that huge meadow – follow the woodland edge on your right gently uphill, then begin to bear left to follow the wire fence ahead, which takes you eventually downhill past the flint quarry again and back to Singleton – or you can take the middle path (dotted on the map), which will take you down the right-hand (eastern) side of Levin Down, a fabulous little nature reserve where much reclamation work is done by volunteers, helping many plants and butterflies to thrive. Turning right at the junction above Charlton will take you back to the original route, where you turn left and back down into Singleton.

Either way – if you have one, a lovely Morris will be waiting to take you home.

South Downs Way

This is one of the most famous walks in Britain. It is about 100 km (62 miles) over Sussex, but the South Downs Way continues officially nearly another 40 km (25 miles) to Winchester. I have walked short distances on hundreds of occasions, but doing the full length I start at Eastbourne via the rail link. You will need to plan overnight stopping places, and food and drink with care.

The long haul out of the town onto the heights of **Beachy Head cliffs**, with its sparkling sea below, is one of life's great uplifts. You can breathe again as you stride the **Seven Sisters**, with their springy turf. Then down to the **Cuckmere River**, with its famous oxbows coiling across flat, egret-haunted meadows, you cross the Cuckmere near Alfriston and climb to the heights of **Firle** at 217 m (713 ft). The views again arguably surpass anything in Britain.

East Sussex has a slightly different climate to West Sussex and Hampshire: it is 'continental', drier and cooler, so the plants are slightly different. Generally, however, you will be walking by 300-plus species of flowering plants all the way, with ten orchid species commonly seen from May to September. This is the best habitat for butterflies in Britain, with forty species in the national list of fifty-eight; those of the blue family are most spectacular – adonis blue, chalkhill blue, common blue, small blue and brown argus among them. Woodlands along the way can have up to forty bird species breeding, from green woodpeckers, to marsh tits, buzzards and red kites, and the open downs have skylarks and stonechats.

Thirty kilometres (20 miles) will be covered by the time you come down to the Ouse crossing at **Southease**. The journey south-west of

Lewes takes you past the early spider orchid site on **Castle Hill,** a national nature reserve. These bare, cool downs with their secret valleys are home to a host of butterflies and chalk flowers. Next is **Ditchling Beacon**, and, after crossing the A23, there is that magnificent escarpment at **Fulking** (*'folc'* means 'folk', as in a people's meeting place). After this you will need even stronger legs, as a number of hills you will encounter are over 200 m (700 ft) high. There is **Chanctonbury**, with its ancient ring and tombs from 3,000 years ago, and after the A24 a long, lonely hill walk to **Amberley**, and the welcome pub and crossing of meandering waters. Back again with the combes below and the Weald beyond, and **Bignor** where the Romans bathed, and the great crossing points with **Stane Street.** Crossing the A272, there is one last acerbic mind-clearing visit to the chalk, the skylarks, the buzzards wheeling and a last look at the eye of the sky before Sussex dissolves at **Buriton.** Make sure you have made a 'get-home' plan: the train from Petersfield is one way, another a lift from your nearest and dearest – in my case in the trusty Morris, both sulking slightly at having been left at home!

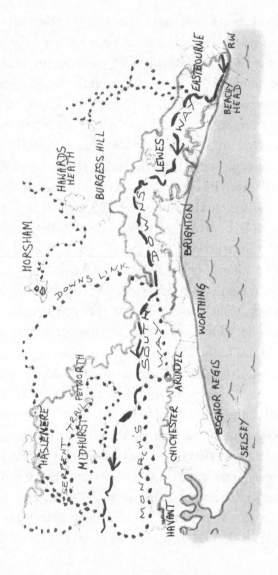

Waterside
Walks

Arun Banks
at Burpham

Here is a pleasant stroll of 4.4 km (2.7 miles) along the Arun banks, suitable for the summer or winter, with a country pub and restaurant at the start and finish.

Parking can be found behind the **George & Dragon** in Burpham, in the large car park at TQ036089.

From here, walk back to the road, turning left, north-west, up the village street, finding a track that runs to the left, past **Old Farriers**, and on downhill to the footpath into the valley. Very soon, to your left, you'll have a view of Arundel

Castle and the grand sweep of the flood plain comes into view. Sheep graze down there, reeds form silver strips in sunlight and wildfowl fly in skeins. It must be one of the loveliest views in Britain. Head downwards to the reeds, which are the tallest native grasses we have. Listen for the moorhen's '*prrruk*' calls from the water; some will patter in weak flight into hiding at your approach. The meadow ahead, with old willows, is home to green woodpeckers, clutching to the dead branches. Walk on to pass the old ruin, which supports a splendid ivy crown in full flower in the winter, attracting late butterflies and hoverflies. Next, turn left onto the Arun banks. You may be amused, as I was, to read the Environment Agency's notices placed on various tiny ditches along this route, which advise against diving or drowning, warning of deep water, slippery surfaces and strong currents.

Keep to the straight and narrow here – but be aware of a real danger next, which is crossing the main railway line. Trains come very fast round bends, so be warned. After crossing, you'll see hawthorn bushes, which always have prolific displays of berries in the autumn and blossom in the spring; I have seen redwings and fieldfares gorging themselves here. The small wood ahead, beyond the river, has a curious name: Foxes Oven. Turning north, South Stoke Church steeple pinpoints the hamlet where the famous brain surgeon H. W. B. Cairns, who attended Lawrence of Arabia after his motorcycle crash in 1935, used to live.

Walk over the stile into the willow woodland and turn right after 20 m, over the footbridge. The woodland here has sedge warblers singing in summer; marsh tits, treecreepers, robins and blackbirds can be seen all year, among many others. Next pass under the railway line, noting the stalactites. A rutted bank path circles left for 500 m, then look for a yellow arrow route going right. The stile you will come to provides a pleasant seat for lunch and for contemplation of the dewberry leaves, and the dangers of diving and drowning, once again, not to speak of 'underwater obstacles'. Trolls, perhaps? From here, cross the meadow heading south-east to the old chalk quarry. Turn right, and right again, over the stile back to the water meadows. Follow the path back to the pub, where awaits the Morris, and the road home, where the dangers of *driving* are real enough.

Bosham to Smugglers Lane

This is one of my Christmas walks (but also good at any time!), around Bosham Harbour and down to Smugglers Lane. It is 7.2 km (4.5 miles).

It's necessary to pay for parking in Bosham village at SU806040. Be warned: free parking, on the foreshore, could drown your car at high tide. Head south to the foreshore and walk left along the cottage footpath if the tide is up, following the road in a right-hand circle. About a hundred brent geese feed here on the bright-green algae, called enteromorpha, from autumn until mid-March. Sometimes little egrets (small white herons), teal (small wild ducks) and redshanks (small waders with orange legs) fly up. Often there is an oystercatcher (black-and-white wader with red beak) looking for tiny crabs near the footpath crossing the muds. Note the clumps of cord grass (also called spartina) growing across the muds. This was accidentally introduced from South America a century ago.

Next head west, but note this road also floods at highest tides. Here you'll see a very nice, wide strip of saltings on your right. Observe the sea rye grass, like cornstalks along the road edge, then the pale grey sea purslane, an almost bushy plant, very close to and following the high-tide mark. The road then bends almost south, then west again, where you may have to take the footpath behind the mini sea wall. At the Saltings House look for a white-and-green metal footpath sign, leading right into the saltings. If this is not possible at high tide, then take the road south to Smugglers Lane. If you are on the Saltings path you will begin to see many more water birds.

Often trips of a hundred dunlin flash up and down the channel here, bright silver in the sunshine. Curlews give spring calls and a cormorant may fly up the channel. You may see tiny crabs washed up, speckled feathers from waders and, at low tide, the lovely sheen of sun on the sinuous channels. Look out for the red clay of brick earth on the foreshore path: also the **1882 Barford & Perkins central land drain sluice gate**, an ancient Victorian artefact with its little brick walls, now sadly about to vanish. As you wander, gaze around at the water and the sky, so as not to miss exciting flights of birds. Soon you will arrive at seats and information boards.

Here I usually sit a while, looking at Itchenor, before returning north and, with the light behind me, enjoy the view far ahead of another top Christmas walk: Kingley Vale. It is beyond the splendid view of the Bosham Church spire. Retrace your steps to the **Bosham Walk Art & Craft Centre** for paintings, beads, sculptures and a cracking good bowl of hot soup. Here I once bought a tiny model of a white Morris Minor, to keep the old girl company, asleep in the car park, safe from the sea.

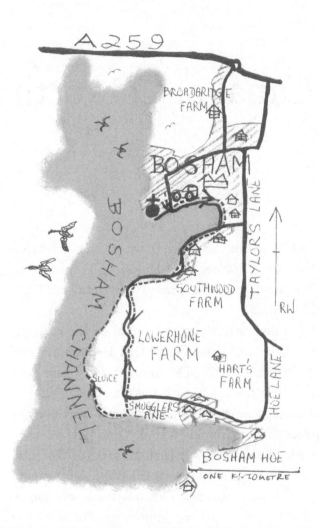

Canal at Colworth

Here the route follows part of the old canal that once connected London to Portsmouth. The walk out and return is a total of 4 km (2.5 miles).

Limited parking can be found on the roadside at Colworth, which is north of Bersted and the A259 at SU913029. The footpath from here goes east, off the road, with the old canal visible in a cottage garden on your right. Note the alder trees showing damp ground. Coming to an open barley field you'll find that all traces of the canal have gone, as it has been filled in, thus erasing part of our history. The canal was completed in 1820, just after the Napoleonic Wars, and at the moment when Beethoven was working on his *Missa Solemnis* and *Ninth Symphony*, which brings the history home to me.

As you walk you'll have views to the left of Halnaker Windmill (AD 1750) and the Trundle Iron Age fort (250 BC). You may hear skylarks singing in the fields here. Continue east, just to the left of a ditch which drains the strawberry field on your right. At the end of the path you'll come back to the remains of the canal. The footpath should then follow the old towpath, but it has not (as yet) been effectively cleared, so may involve wading through nettles. Anyway, soon after you can climb out of the field and onto the towpath proper. To your left is that dinosaur of waste management, a landfill site, which has been wired off, but the firm has planted a very good hedge to screen this monstrosity of our present historical age (AD 1988) and mown the towpath footpath, so it is a very pleasant walk.

I did, on one occasion, hear a rare sound here: the song of a lesser whitethroat. Note also sedge warblers, blackcap warblers and chiffchaffs; linnets also breed here. Butterflies to be found include ringlet, meadow brown, comma, whites and common blue, which breed on the copious amounts of bird's foot trefoil. Goldfinches feed on the teasels. I have also found a rare grass for Sussex in the bottom of the canal: wood small-reed *(Calamagrostis epigejos)*, which is up to 2 m tall; also agrimony, hardhead, willowherb and bullrush. Look out for signs that a roebuck has marked his fraying stocks, and for where badgers have dug out wasps' nests and foxes have caught rabbits.

One can stop for lunch where another footpath joins the route from the north; there is a pleasant open patch of grass here with honeysuckle. Greenfinches sing from the top branches of an old oak and a tame chaffinch might come for your crumbs. After this retrace your steps to Colworth (Cula's homestead, AD 600), much pleased with your brief encounter with nature and history. I return to my old Morris (AD 1963).

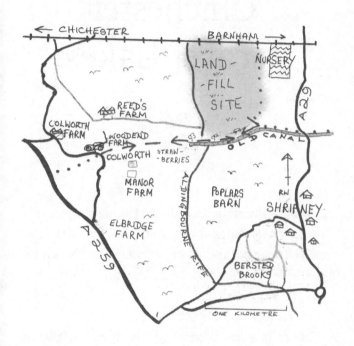

Chichester
Gravel Lakes

A walk around the 'lake district' is always pleasant – especially when it is actually in Chichester, or rather near it. The old gravel works on the south-east side of the city make a nice walk – best in the spring, but don't feel inhibited by other seasons – of 4.5 km (2.7 miles).

There is a small parking bay at SU877039, on the Runcton road just south of the A27/A259 roundabout, off the south-eastern sector. From here, walk south along a hard way between **Peckham Lake** to your right and **Leythorne Lake** to your left. Nearly every lake has a pair of great crested grebes, which have a wonderful courting display before settling down to nest; they display 'Elizabethan ruffs' around their necks and have very pointed beaks. Grebes swim low down in the water, but when presenting wedding gifts of weed to each other they rise upwards and even seem to stand on the water. Their nests are low slumps of wet weed hidden among bushes, just an inch or two above the water. Other birds here are coots, black with white porcelain-like frontal lobes; they make slightly taller piles of weed.

Soon you will come to Vinnetrow Lake, then Runcton Lake. Coming to the bungalow conurbation of former car-breakers brings you close to New Lake: this is one of the best lakes because of its shelter and it is worth lingering with binoculars alert. New Lake is one of the few places south of the London reservoirs where that rare sawbill duck, the smew, with its superb white plumage with black tracings, is seen in cold winters. Other sawbills have included mergansers and even goosanders in the past. Certainly you should see the gadwall duck here, and also tufted and pochard ducks. Rafts are placed here for use of common terns for nesting in summer.

Next, turn sharply right, north-west, to find **Copse Lake** on your right, followed by the enormous **Ivy Lake**. **Trout Lake** is on the left. The reeds here give cover to thousands of swallows and sand martins in the autumn, and are good swooping areas for insects in the summer. Breeding from spring and on to summer will be reed warblers, reed buntings, and even kingfishers, and the very secretive water rail – just a small selection of the birds you might see on the lakes. Look especially in the spring for black terns, which pass through here on migration.

I usually walk until I'm opposite the convent and then retrace my steps, looking to check if birds seen are still there – or if new ones have appeared – and back to the beginning, where I see the old Morris, not quite as white as the mute swans on these lakes, but born in 1963, just that little bit older than the oldest, which even so might be forty.

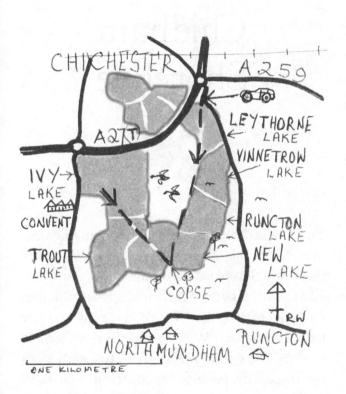

CHICHESTER

A 259

A 27(T)

LEYTHORNE
LAKE

VINNETROW
LAKE

IVY →
LAKE

CONVENT

RUNCTON
LAKE

NEW
LAKE

TROUT →
LAKE

COPSE

RW

RUNCTON

NORTH MUNDHAM

ONE KILOMETRE

133

Chidham
Shoreline

This is a brilliant seaside walk of 8 km (5 miles): take before mid-March to see waterfowl, before they leave Sussex for the Arctic.

In the car, take the A259, turning down Chidham Lane and parking at SU794035 in the bay kept tidy by parish council. Walk east to the shore for 300 m, then follow the shoreline south (the path along the shore may become impassable at high tides) down the west side of Bosham Channel. To the ancients, Bosham Harbour looked like a sort of moneybag which filled up twice a day. The Old English word for pouch was '*ceode*', which became '*chid*'; '*ham*' could mean 'watery meadow' as well as the more usual 'village'. Follow the shoreline with sea purslane (grey-blue-green leathery leaves), sea wormwood and sea aster. Brent geese feed across the muds at low tide (they leave mid-March) together with redshank (red legs): teal, our smallest duck, are here, plus a few shelduck (big, white with black-and-brown markings) and dunlin, which are very small whitish waders creeping about like mice just ahead of the tide. There are about twenty-five different species of waterfowl commonly seen along this shore, not including various species of gull. Look for little egrets, now established due to warmer weather in general – about 200 live in the harbour complex.

At **Cullimer's Pond**, the path moves about 50 m inland, where you should continue south to avoid the slipways and pass **Cobnor House**, which was built in 1820. This was home to Martin Beale OBE, a well-known farmer, yachting Olympiad and benefactor. Look for his memorial seat when the path turns at **Cobnor Point**. The shoreline path may now be underwater. **Stakes Island**, which can be seen to your left, was an ancient embankment to reclaim Thorney Channel: now a refuge for breeding gulls and terns. Here ancient

135

oak trees cling to land with tenacious roots like octopuses. Once, in this spot, a Stuka dive-bomber crashed at the height of the Battle of Britain on 18 August, 1940. Butcher's broom and stinking iris grow under the trees hereabouts. The path on the sea wall or shore continues north for another mile to Chidham Point. The mudflats here are a good place to see wigeon, also red-breasted mergansers, goldeneye (both are diving duck), avocets, brent geese and other waders. Note the pretty stag's horn plantain atop the sea wall.

Next, turn east on the yellow arrow route into fields where roe deer splodge in wet ground. Turn right (south) when you reach the road. St Mary's Church has a splendid brass eagle lectern; plain thirteenth century, but restored in 1864. At the corner walk south into the fields, following a ditch that grows the seaside umbellifer called Alexanders, with peppery seeds in the autumn. In the spring primroses grow on the ditch's sides. The path then goes left past Chidmere Pond, where there should be tufted duck and pochard. Bitterns have often been seen here, too, in the winter. Continue back to the car park: I return as ever to the Morris, white with the same brown markings as a shelduck.

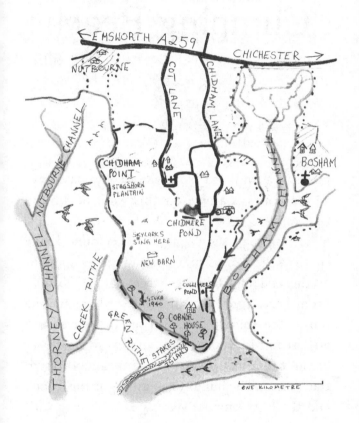

Climping Beach

Here is a walk to blow your cobwebs away. Three hours is ample for this walk of 3.6 km (2.2 miles).

Parking (pay and display) can be found 1 mile south of the A259, 2 miles west of Littlehampton, at the end of Climping Street, at TQ005007. From here, turn to walk westwards along the top of the shingle bank, to see the waves and any seabirds about, but also a footpath to begin with, just inside the bank and through the bushes. The hungry sea gnaws at this beach and the Environment Agency is kept busy with groynes, boulder breakwaters and capping the bank with more shingle. Most of this walk is on firm ground, but you may find the occasional place where you have to scramble because of erosion. The first thing to notice is the variety of seaside plants, which increases as you walk west, with a grand finale at the further end near Poole Place. Obvious first are the tamarisk bushes near a lone oak that looks like an umbrella. Sea beet grows all along this walk – once used as a cooked vegetable, today too rare to be picked. Here also grows orache (fat-hen to gardeners and farmers) with a possible four species along this coast; ox-eye daisies are here, too. Then, growing out of the old flint sea wall, you may spot a nice line of sea rye grass and even a clump of marram, that binder of the sand.

Watch the sea for travellers: terns till October, Mediterranean gulls and little gulls are all possible among the common, black-headed, herring and lesser black-back; also brent geese skimming low over the water. Skua and sea duck may all be passing a little further out. Stop and sit at the first big pile of rocks – a useful place to have your sandwiches – and note the swarms of sand hoppers on which turnstones will be feeding. If you keep very still they will take no notice of you. Look in season for the clumps of quite extraordinary yellow sea-horn poppy, growing under the green public footpath signs. Then see many more on a wonderful wide lawn, in which you will find birdsfoot trefoil, rock samphire, yellow medic, bristly ox-tongue, wild carrot and scarlet pimpernel. Look especially for large clumps of sea kale, once a delicacy in London restaurants, now protected.

Turn now and retrace your steps. At high tide small trips of wading birds roost here in the bay between breakwaters; you should see oystercatchers, ring plovers, sanderlings and yet more turnstone. Because of the usually rough sea, the colours of the ocean's arm are especially brilliant along this unsheltered walk and you will feel completely invigorated at the end. If you wear spectacles you will find them frosted with the salt spray, as was the Morris windscreen when I returned.

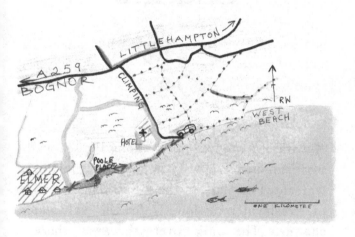

Fishbourne Channel

A walk of 6 km (3.8 miles) along the sea walls of Fishbourne shows you some of the finest waterfowl displays in the UK; this is because of freshwater inflows into the salt-water channel. The walk covers the area where I make the official national wildfowl counts every winter.

Parking is possible in the area near St Mary's Church (SU842045), reached by a right turn on a (fairly blind) corner on the byroad turning left off the A259, off the A27 bypass roundabout west of Chichester. From this area, proceed north up a small path towards the church: a plain thirteenth-century specimen, restored in 1877, with fourteenth-century tiles on the altar step, triple lancets and Purbeck shafts. Turning left, continue west on the path around the edge of the field and an old streambed to the sea wall. If walking during high tide and in the winter, the first birds you may note are some 400 wigeon. There are up to twenty species of waterbirds at least in the winter, including about a hundred mute swans.

Turn north to follow the sea wall paths to the millpond at the top of the channel: beware, as this can be soggy in places. Look for kingfishers at the freshwater sluices. Near the reed beds note several hundred waders and wild duck resting at high tide on the old salthouse wall, now grassed over; curlew, grey plover, dunlin, ring plover, black-tailed godwit, redshank, wigeon, teal and golden-eye duck should also be found. Low tide takes them back into the muds to feed. Moorhens and water-rails can be spotted around the reed beds as well. A raised bridge will take you over the stream, then follow the narrow path beside the stream and adjacent gardens. Passing the millpond you will see mallards, gadwall ducks, a pair of little grebes, coots and moorhens. Follow the path over the sluice and through the reed beds – note that at highest tides this can be flooded for up to an hour, sometimes to the depth of 1 m, so time your walk to get through well before high tide – then it will have gone down by the time you return.

The walk down the west bank of the channel gives an even better display of up to 2,000 birds; check the meadows to the west for grazing birds such as brent geese and curlews. The way is easy to begin with but it has one or two difficult places further south, which need care to negotiate. Eventually you come to a small oak grove where a pond may, if you are lucky, show a perching kingfisher – this is a sheltered spot useful for eating sandwiches. Refreshed, you should now retrace your steps north back along the sea wall. Although the scene is the same you are now going the opposite way and it will all appear very different. Kingley Vale can be seen in the distance, along with the spire of the cathedral; cloudscapes here can be spectacular. You may see up to about ten herons and twenty little egrets – white as my Morris, which is just as nippy and neat.

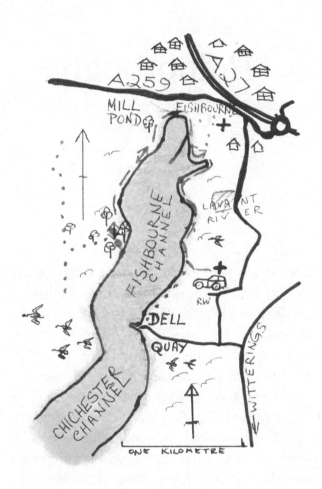

Pulborough
Brooks

This is another of my favourite walks in our county, with a distance of 5.2 km (3.3 miles). If possible, go on a Sunday, otherwise you'll have to work out Horsham RDC's awkward parking arrangements for Pulborough at TQ053186, which involves getting a token from nearby shops.

Exit the parking area down the steps on the west side, walking sharply left down the lane to some lovely meadows with wonderful views to the Downs. Coming to the Arun banks, a footbridge over the tiny River Stor takes you straight into one of the finest RSPB nature reserves in Britain.

Lazy rivers, reedy ditches, herds of cattle in the distance, and the chirrups of reed buntings and sedge warblers in the spring and summer make this a soothing ramble. Look out for vestiges of an old Roman road over what was at that time a swamp.

Leave the Arun and bear left over meadows, noting clumps of dark green rushes (soft rush and compact rush). Another stile leads into a sandy lane, uphill past a big old willow and with teasels along the way. Look for RSPB Little Hanger hide under a big oak to the left – it has lots of pictures of birds on the walls, and offers a good view onto one of the reserve scrapes, with waders, ducks and swans. The walk now runs south-east, diagonally across rabbit-grazed meadows, then left at the next stile eastward, sticking to the wooden footpath fingerpost route. You'll come across a small healthy pond in the dip, then walk through bushy meadows which are designed for breeding song birds and migrants. I have heard whitethroat warblers, blackcap warblers and chichaffs. Note the snowberry bushes, too, to the left of the path.

Soon you'll arrive at the tiny Wigginholt Church, built in about 1400 for 'yeoman farmers, shepherds and herdsmen of the wildbrooks'. It was upgraded somewhat in 1859 with a splendid east window, although most are early perpendicular; forty-three species of flowers reside in the churchyard. Keep left, walking around the old rectory wall to continue northward through the meadows, over stiles, past donkeys, then down the steps to **Bankside Cottage**, with its unforgettable view over the marshes to the west. What sunsets they must get in the waters – it is like the Camargue.

Follow the edge of the brooks, dropping sometimes into a rue where elder and wild plums grow. Cross the River Stor again, at a Siamese-twin-like oak, which is weeping with sap on its unhappy hip joint and will one day crash to the ground in a gale. Bear right to another stile and follow the path back north, past Brook Gate Farm to the main road, where you should turn left along the pavement back to the car park. The proximity to the A283 is not especially salubrious, but it makes you appreciate the slow and quiet country of the brooks you have just been through (although it makes my token-toting Traveller a bit tetchy).

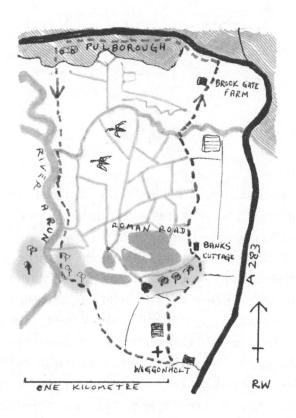

PULBOROUGH

BROOK GATE
FARM

RIVER ARUN

ROMAN ROAD

BANKS
COTTAGE

A 283

WIGGONHOLT

ONE KILOMETRE

RW

River Arun

I personally get a flavour of the Norfolk Broads of my boyhood haunts with this lovely walk of 6.5 km (4 miles) along the Arun banks.

Parking can be found in Arundel near the old road bridge (TQ020070): pay-and-display car parks are either side of the bridge and there's free parking, if you can find an empty place, on the roadside east of the castle. Starting on the south side of the bridge, take the footpath eastwards along the south bank of the Arun and walk between houses and onto a slightly muddy bank top, where you immediately smell the salt tide which makes the Arun the sixth fastest-flowing river in England.

Follow this path around two enormous meanders for the next 4 km (2.5 miles). This gives you the best view of the castle, with the cathedral to the left and the river in front. It is one of the most splendid of all English views. On the other side the steep wooded hill called **Offham Hanger** comes into view. In front of it you can see the famous **Arundel Wildfowl & Wetlands Trust reserve**, which gives rise to many birds, such as herons, mallards, moorhens and reed warblers. Straight ahead, as you walk close to the railway line, is **Camp Hill** on the downland fields. Stay on the bank path as you pass a white house – note a broken old ash tree riddled by woodpeckers, after passing through the small gate. The water meadows here have both soft and hard rush clumps; there ought to be snipe breeding here but I have never heard a single bleat. Observe the orange leaves of osiers, green of willow and grey of sallows around the wildfowl collection.

Arriving at a point opposite the **Black Rabbit pub**, which always looks very picturesque and inviting, makes you glad you brought your lunch, because you can't get over the river unless you swim! Note the wreck of an old boat, which must have an interesting history. The railway has to be crossed soon – remember these trains are very fast and quiet. Safely across, continue for 250 m, then turn sharply right along a raised causeway, with a nice curved blackthorn hedge next to you on your left, in which I've seen long-tailed tits. Head for the Lombardy poplars just left of castle in the distance, to find a stile which leads you into a very pleasant hedge track back to the white house. There are lots of wrens, robins, marsh tits and dunnocks here. Turn right at Crossing Cottage to cross the line again, then left, back along the same riverbank, to the town. Here I see the old Morris, which looked uncommonly like an old mother swan sitting there, her wooden frame like varnished reed stems. Her exhaust is a bit of a reedy warbler, too.

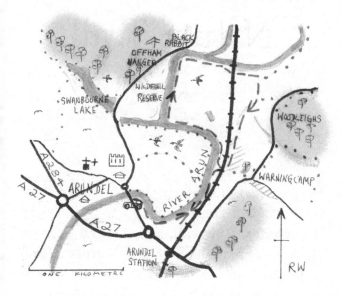

Sidlesham Ferry Nature Trail

Here we have a beautiful little summer stroll (or perhaps a breezier one in the winter) by the saltings. The walk runs around Pagham Harbour's Sidlesham Ferry Nature Trail, a leaflet for which is obtainable at the information centre and car park on the Selsey road at SZ857967. The walk is 2.5 km (1.6 miles).

Set off on the path heading south, noting the masses of teasels and common mallow around and about. A bird hide situated on your on right overlooks the famous **Ferry Pool**, which will have a daily change of rare and common waterbirds. Look especially for the occasional curlew sandpiper in August, green sandpipers in July and shelduck in the summer, when the ducklings of different ages may be guarded by one or two 'aunties', while the remainder of the parents go to Bridgewater Bay in Somerset to moult (holiday rest?!). Some parents go to Heligoland in the Baltic. Lapwings and redshanks are usually seen around the edge of the pool most times of the year. There will be mallard ducklings in the summer, too, and in the winter our smallest duck, the teal, which breeds in eastern Europe. Birds come and go continually at this secure feeding and watering place. Usually the day's sightings are written up at the visitor centre.

Go left at the Ferry Channel, with its roaring water siphons, then follow the track of the ancient Selsey tramway north-eastward along the edge of Pagham Harbour nature reserve. Here wonderful views across the sand and mudflats, which of course are covered twice daily by the tide, can be had. If walking during low tide, observe the lush meadows of sea cordgrass (*Spartina*), which was introduced accidentally to Britain a century ago. In the distance you might spy egrets and oystercatchers. In the winter you can enjoy good views of brent geese and wigeon, and in the summer note the shoreline plants below you, for example, sea spurrey with star-like flowers. There are half a dozen seats down this route dedicated to birdwatchers whose happy haunt this was when they were alive.

As the path bends north-west you'll see a very fine acre or two of salting on your right; with its broken sea walls it's very attractive, with varying colours of green which would have inspired Matisse. Thick hedges of wild plum, blackthorn, hawthorn, elder and blackberry line the way here, in which greenfinches, blackbirds, robins and hedge sparrows live. Butterflies to be seen here include red admiral, hedge brown and holly blue. After arriving at the road, with the **Crab & Lobster pub and restaurant** to the right, turn immediately left past an old mill pond with its moorhens, coots, mallards, reed and sedge warblers. At **Island Cottage** turn left onto the public footpath to cross an old hay meadow with Yorkshire fog grass.

The path then follows an old sea wall again, under sheltering hedges, when you may see blue and long-tailed tits and willow warblers in the summer. Steps to your left lead back to the beginning, where I spot an old Morris Traveller, white as a shelduck – or an egret – perhaps an avocet? Just as rare.

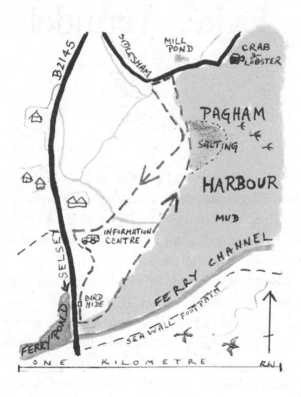

Swanbourne Lake, Arundel

This is one of the most popular walks in Sussex. A hundred thousand people each year visit Swanbourne Lake and you can see why. The stroll of 1.8 km (1.2 miles) is through shady woods, with a view of the lake below almost all the way.

Masses of free parking can be found along the stately lime avenue road at TQ020075, on the east side of Arundel Castle. Fine weekends bring most of the visitors here and most tend to walk anti-clockwise from the small buffet and restaurant at the lake entrance. I prefer to go clockwise. There is a hard, wide path almost all the way; cycles are not permitted, so walking is comfortable. I set off north-west on the southern flank of the lake, near the trout-feeding centre. A clear-water stream feeds the lake from the surrounding chalk hills, so when in good health this water has a lovely pale-blue tinge. The lake dried up in 1976 and 1996, but since then the Environment Agency has dredged it and Southern Water has agreed to reduce the water extraction at the Madehurst borehole by 66 per cent, which has secured the flow. The lake was used 1,000 years ago to drive a mill. Constable painted Arundel Mill and Castle in 1837 and was still working on his masterpiece the day he died.

As you progress, note the masses of wild waterfowl below you. Some are overspill from the Wildfowl & Wetlands Trust centre nearby. A hundred coots gather near the restaurant to be fed; moorhens chirrup and show their white tails as threats to each other – sometimes they battle with their long claws. Take note also of several little grebes. An unusual duck, which is easily seen here, is the gadwall – these are sandy brown and have a black tail area. You are also likely to see pochards, the males with conker-coloured heads, tufted ducks, cormorants and black-headed gulls. The steep woodland grows box, some ancient beeches with 'Gollum' roots and a spectacular display of hart's tongue ferns.

Turn right at the end to return along the east bank of the lake. Here you come into the open chalk grassland of **Arundel Park**, part of the whole Site of Special Scientific Interest (SSSI) plot. There are lots of butterflies here in the summer and flowers include rock rose and sweet woodruff – look out for the holly oaks, too. You can buy corn to feed the ducks and geese at the end of this walk, and there are a few seats to rest on and even some small white rowing boats to hire, before enjoying the trip home – for me, in a white Morris: the perfect end to a picnic.

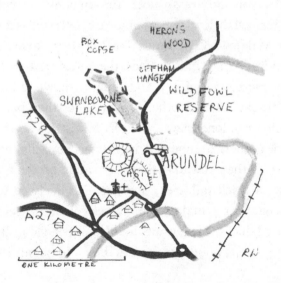

Thorney Island

This is one of my most favourite walks and for many years one that my family and I always took on Boxing Day (although it has other attractions in the summer months). The walk is 11.5 km (7.2 miles) in length, along the footpath around Thorney Island.

Limited parking can be had outside Thornham Lane sewage works at SU757049 (or, alternatively, at Emsworth car parks, meaning you'll have to adjust your starting point on the map). From the sewage works cross the road, taking the footpath west (if it's impassable there is a private tarmac road you could use) to the sea wall and the **Sussex Border Path,** turning south. If you stay on top of the sea wall you can look down into **Little Deep** reed beds with coots, tufted ducks, mallards, moorhens and bearded tits in the reed tassels.

After this come the **Eames Farm** meadows, often with flocks of brent geese, in the winter, and herons around the pond. You will soon arrive at the **Great Deep**, an old arm of the sea, landlocked since 1870 but flushed out twice daily by a tidal sluice. This is the winter shelter for gatherings of shelduck, oystercatchers, wigeon and redshanks during high tides; parties of little grebes bob down underwater and the small creek running north-east is where little egrets, greenshanks, teal and snipe feed. Next, you need to get through the Ministry of Defence gate using the intercom – they may ask for your mobile phone number and postcode. You must stay on footpath marked by yellow arrow posts throughout. Here you can enjoy brilliant scenes in sunshine of blue tide or blue-gleaming mudflats, speckled with blackish strands of sea-wrack, and trips of tiny silver birds feeding along the edge of the tide are dunlin. At high tide these birds gather in a large flock at Pilsey Island, our halfway point.

After **Marker Point** the vast open spaces of **Pilsey Sands** stretch south, a true wilderness. Here you'll pass by sheltering thorn hedges, some superbly shaped by the sea-thrown gales. Look out for stonechats in the gorse – also here is a small brick bird-hide. At **Longmere Point** pass **Pilsey Island**, a local nature reserve leased by the RSPB from the MOD, enlarged in recent years due to tides sweeping sand from East Head across the bay. Here you may observe the twisting aerial display of thousands of dunlin. The path now turns north, up the eastern side of Thorney. Note the old runways and grass meadows where brent and curlew often feed. Pass the complex of service houses and the slipway, and come to **St Nicholas's Church**, founded nine centuries ago, with airmen remembered from Word War Two. The skyline to the right shows Chichester Cathedral, Bosham Church, and Kingley Vale. Shoreline plants here include sea purslane, forming soft grey bushes; the muds feed small flocks of grey plover, dunlin, redshank and curlew.

Contact the MOD through the intercom to the exit gate at the eastern sluice of **Great Deep** (you might spot a kingfisher here), continue then, bearing left over the stile, on the footpath to some houses and boatyard at **Prinsted Point**, and on into Thornham Lane. I am welcomed by the Morris with salt-frosted windscreen from the sea wind.

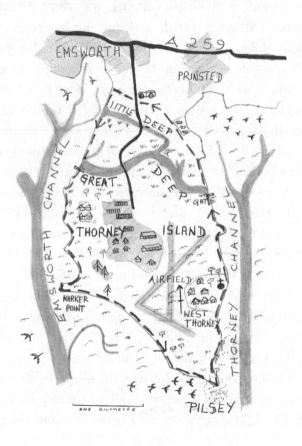

West Wittering

This harbour walk of 4.5 km (2.8 miles) is intended to show you one of the best wetlands on the south coast, combining at least four inter-related habitats in such a small area, all with attendant birds with specialised feeding habits. I often take the walk in the winter; it is different but equally good in the summer.

Pay and park at West Wittering beach (SZ 777984), next to the cafe and lavatories. This will give you the opportunity to walk slowly north-west along grassland towards East Head. Inland, the meadows are grazed by flocks of brent geese during the winter months: up to 1,000 birds gently cronkling their own messages.

If disturbed, the geese will rise in magnificent unison. I have also seen 200 ruffs here during spring passage, one of the red letter days of my life. You may also see the large flock of golden plovers that spends the winter here and on fields farther along this walk.

Turn right to follow the path along the sea wall, or the shingle beach if it's low tide, up the east side of the tidal lagoon. East Head sand dunes protect this salt marsh, making it a haven for many feeding waterfowl. Teal and shelduck can be found in the creeks here, as can curlews, redshanks, dunlin, oystercatchers, lapwings, grey plovers and other waders, between September and March. Note the rice grass sticking up out of the mud hillocks (an invasive South American species brought here in the 1900s). Snow Hill meadows to the right provide brackish pools for these species, and also for avocets and godwits.

There is a fragment of seaside heath at Roman Landing with sheep sorrel and gorse. The footpath, heading north to Ella Nore, takes you past the farm fields on which golden plover often feed or rest from October to March; other waders also use these fields as a mass roost during high tides. The view north-west across channel to

Pilsey Sands may reward you with eider duck, or red-throated or black-throated divers, as these deep-sea divers drift with the tide. Next the path turns east, past Ella Nore shingle spit with its dense beds of sea purslane and shingle flora. Turn right again into Ella Nore Lane, with another grandstand view of all those golden plover – there may be more than 1,000 here. Turn right when you reach the road (remembering that 100 m on your right at the main road junction is Sir Henry Royce's old house 'Camacha', and the studio where he designed cars and Spitfire engines).

Continue up the lane to the **St Peter & St Paul's Church** gate and take the footpath through the churchyard, over the stile through meadows back to Snow Hill, and then continue down the sea wall again past those lovely marshes, now on your left. You can almost see it all from the front seat of a strategically parked car – for me, the Morris, although the heater is a bit feeble in winter. I bet Sir Henry never had a Morris.

Woodland
Walks

Charlton Forest

This is a super down and forest walk of 8 km (5 miles), with gentle climbs for the first half, then downhill to the end – which is as it should be.

You'll find parking on the roadside in a small bay in Charlton village at SU887131. Now walk a short way back towards Singleton, finding a stile in the hedge on your right, for the crossing of a sheep-grazed meadow uphill onto Levin Down Nature Reserve. Pause at the seat to Brenda Wyrill at the top, from which you can admire the view west to Bow Hill, south-west to the Trundle and east up the Lavant Valley, reminiscent of the Derbyshire Dales. Levin Down is grazed by Herdwick sheep, which sometimes resemble cherubims. Keep right along the hillside, heading north.

Approaching a lone pine, note the splendid lichen-rich turf here *(Cladonia spp)* and the mature and young cushions of ling *(Calluna vulgaris)*, which the careful management of this reserve has preserved as a rare chalk-heath community. You'll come to another smaller seat along here, from which you can enjoy Green Hill, to the east. The reserve here in the summer is filled with butterflies, wild orchids and downland flowers – also the rare juniper grows here. Head over the stile and into the woodland, where you'll see robins, blackbirds, long-tailed tits and turtle doves in the summer.

Once you arrive at the open downs follow the yellow arrow route north-east for 330 m to a metal gate. You'll pass a 1972 direction post, dedicated to the famous 1738 Charlton Hunt. Continue for about 25 m east to a vehicle track, then turn sharply left onto a grassy track between two wire fences. Head down the rue into the valley to the forest. The entry point is called Burntoak Gate. Keeping the gnarled beech tree to your left, take the blue arrow route north, avoiding four other rides radiating from this point. Walk uphill twixt spruce, cypress and pines, and cross the Bronze Age field lynchets; then cross the gravel road and five-crossway. Pollard willows line the path here – they keep the deer from getting at the young pines.

Arriving at the five-crossway, branch half-right along the obvious walkers' path. After 450 m turn sharply right on the yellow arrow route south-east, back through the forest of young beech on your left and cypresses on your right. Walk straight over the six-crossway, on for a further 1 km until you drop down to where a forest barn is becoming derelict in a dell. Here turn right, down North Lane, on the blue arrow route. Note an ancient oak in the hedge on the right, which is badly damaged – it was set alight by troops in last war and twenty sten-gun bullets are embedded in the dead wood. Follow the lane back to Charlton – where I return to my cherubic Morris – noting the fine tall hazel hedge bordering the road.

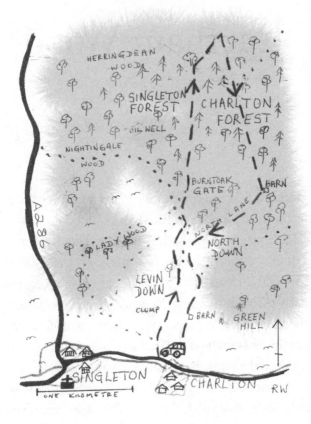

Eartham Wood

Here is a 5-km (3-mile) walk to see autumn colours in the beech forests of Eartham.

Parking can be found at the Eartham Wood Forestry Commission car park, off the A285 at SU939107. Head east out of the car park, along the path through a young Norway spruce plantation, then go left on the wide hard gravel track northwards for just under 1 km – after 20 m note a splendid spindle bush on your left. There are lots more native shrubs to see: hazel, hawthorn, willow, oak, ash, dogwood, beech, birch and brambles, making this a good butterfly spot in the summer.

Next you will come to the old government amenity plantings of the 1950s – an effort to

make beech monoculture more acceptable;
bird cherry and Norway maple are also among
them. The monoculture has some of the best
maiden beech plantings you will see anywhere:
tall, straight, slender, healthy and with golden
crowns. They are an absolute picture and ought
to win the Turner Prize. Keep walking straight
ahead, where the gravel road turns right near
a small male holly bush on the left, and start
climbing slightly uphill. Note the small, fine,
rush scattered along this path – it is slender-
rush, introduced from North America a century
ago. Look out for a sweet chestnut grove on
your left, behind some low banks, where the soil
thins, the beech become scraggy and wood tor
grass begins to show itself.

Turn right at the top of the hill onto the
bridleway, where the soil changes to clay with
flints, so the beeches recover. Next, go right
at the post and rails onto the blue arrow route
and start downhill, south-east, onto a sunny
grass ride. Note several old fallow buck rutting
stands here, some which have really bruised
the odd dogwood bush. Here you'll get a brief
view ahead to Littlehampton, before you pass
a large male yew tree. At the crossrides look

out for a rare pendulous beech covered with ivy and note also the weld growing on the crossride. Walk on to the valley bottom, with its deer hide and another male yew tree, also with pinhead flowers ready to burst in February.

Next you'll arrive at the Roman road of Stane Street and also Monarch's Way, along which Charles II is said to have fled to France. There's a nice picnic seat here at the seven-crossway. Walk south-west down the Roman road towards Halnaker, just over 1 km to the car park and I to my little old Morris, patient as a Cavalier for the return of its driver. Take note of the American red oaks along this glorious English Appian Way, happily without any strung-up martyrs, as were once seen along the original one leading to Rome – and even more happily without the princely Charles having ever been seen hanging here, or I would never have been born (I am a descendant of Charles II and Nell Gwynn, through my mother's forebears) –but that is another story!

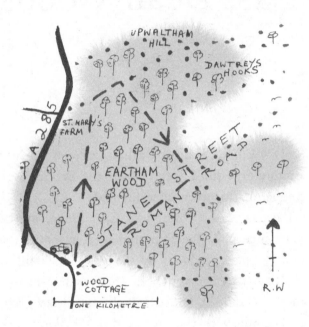

East Dean Woods

This 4-km (2.5-mile) walk takes you up into remote and quiet areas where the Bronze Age people of this area once farmed.

Parking can be found in East Dean, at the very nice pub, the Star and Garter, or in the church park hidden by hedges (SU904129). All Saints is twelfth to thirteenth century, modified in 1870, but still small, and flinty grey, in keeping with the village. Look inside to see the ancient bell clappers and their bronze bushes now replaced: also the famous local poet and playwright Christopher Fry's verse on them.

Look on the south-east outside wall for a curious tombstone, dated 1688, dedicated to a blacksmith named Peachy. The churchyard has 127 species of flowering plants. Then, walk north-west into a deep, narrow lane to a metal gate with a clasping chain, and through into the downland meadow. Shortly after, leave the main track to bend sharply right on the blue arrow route, following the deep grass track northward, up the steep hill. Note the fine downland on the banks, especially the bird's foot trefoil, yellow medic and sheep's fescue grass. At the top you'll find a stile with a seat and verse: 'Field, coppice, cottage and all I see. Vivified, hallowed, by memory. A. E. West, copse-man and countryman.'

Walk onwards and upwards into the driftway, with its thick hedges of holly, hawthorn, hazel, spindle, dogwood, blackthorn, elder, ash, bramble, field maple and wild rose. Shortly after you'll come to a yellow arrow pointing north-west, half left, into wheat field – aim for almost the left hedge of the right-hand wood. (Alternatively, walk in a half-circle all around the edge of this field.) The going is flinty and requires boots, or you will bend your ankle. Arriving at Scratlee Wood, follow its edge until it crosses your path and you enter – just before this entry there is a pleasant triangle of wood brome grassland where you can lunch. Stock doves and jackdaws here tell of the big ancient beeches, and their holes and crevices.

Cross the Bronze Age field-banks and come to a cross-tracks where you should turn right on the yellow arrow route. Note the profusion of dog's mercury and herb bennet here. In the young beech plantation you'll come to a five-crossway, where you should veer right onto a vehicle trackway, where many spotted orchids appear in June. After 180 m double back right, south-west, on the blue arrow route, along the steep slope of Pond Barn combe, staying on this track until you come back to the wheat field. Walking along the edge of the field takes you back south to where you crossed the wheat earlier. Then head back to East Dean and the beginning, where I know the Morris, like the bells, also has new Bronze Age bearings.

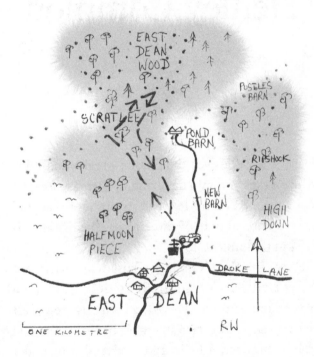

EAST DEAN WOOD

POSTLES BARN

SCRATLEE

POND BARN

RIPSHOCK

NEW BARN

HIGH DOWN

HALFMOON PIECE

DROKE LANE

EAST DEAN

ONE KILOMETRE

RW

Henley Common

Here is a walk over the Sussex greens and hills, which takes you into dark and mysterious forests. For this one be sure to wear strong footwear and keep a careful note of directions. The distance is 5.5 km (3.4 miles).

Park in the National Trust car park for **Woolbeding Common** (SU869261), which is on a very minor road. There's a fabulous view west here, even before you start. To begin, walk east uphill, between a holly and a silver birch, under some power cables, joining a sunken way, until you come to a left turn on a fingerpost by two old beech trees. Here is a lofty avenue of beech, birch and oak. After 400 m, at **Pine Hill House**, a sign points left, but keep going straight on along a narrow path, noting bilberry plants around your ankles. Now comes the difficult bit: the path vanishes. Just slither downhill through the trees until you come to a road, and Oak Cottage.

Here, go right on the yellow arrow route, on New Lipchis Way, into a tall-fir wood along a broad forest track. Note the hard ferns here, small and rather like moth-eaten quills – also liverworts and thick blankets of moss. This area is a cool sanctuary of green silence; the tall firs often have goldcrests feeding at the tops. At the chestnut coppice a footpath goes left, but carry straight on. The ground may become soggy, with a causeway. The track then bears left, downhill, before beginning a long right-hand curve, eventually coming to a meadow. Cross this meadow downhill, keeping an old oak 10 m to your left, where you'll come to some lumps of invasive foreign Himalayan balsam; the path then winds through this into the wood. Just after a pond, turn left on the yellow arrow route. Join the road at Stable Cottage, just after which is a nice trunk-stool on which to sit for lunch. You may see scores of white pheasants here, looking like egrets or gulls.

At **Willow Cottage**, a little further along, turn right down the road, over the bridge and then cross the dangerous A286 into a wood, to follow the footpath south-west, uphill and parallel to the main road. Cross the road again at **Horseshoe House**, another very dangerous crossing, making for **Verdley Edge**. The track climbs to a yellow arrow pointing right. After 300 m leave the broad track and head uphill in the gulley on the yellow arrow route to the left. Note the phenomenal moss blankets here, as in rainforests. At the top, after a brief view north into Linchmere Ridge, turn sharply left, then right along a farm track. Coming to a meadow point yourself at **Scotland Farmhouse**, due west, then pass it to the right. Heading back into the woods, follow the track around to the left, meeting a large track where you should turn right, soon coming back to that avenue of beech trees. Turn left to return downhill and to the start; where I spot the Morris, which smugly thinks it has had the best of the day enjoying a tremendous sunset from the car park.

ONE KILOMETRE

Huckswood, Compton

This is an easy, pleasant walk of, 5.6 km (3.4 miles) through downland fields, lanes and yew woods with lots of deer, badgers and woodland birds around you, as well as bluebells and primroses.

There is some very limited unofficial roadside parking for two cars along the byroad between Compton and Finchdean at SU758147. From here start northwards through a woodland rue and into a cereal field, with magnificent yew, ivy and holly hedges all around. Go through the gap in the hedge and continue north across another

field to Huckswood Lane, where you should
turn left, west, leaving the bridlepath. This is a
mature rue with old oaks, beech and yews: also
old hazel coppice, spindle, whitebeam and ash are
here, as are lords and ladies (*Arum maculatum*),
and violet. After 450 m there is a ruin, perhaps
an old barn, as you pass Huckswood Copse to
the left, and cross into Hampshire. Views open
out to the left ahead, to Idsworth and Chalton
Downs, above the main railway line between
Portsmouth and London. Mistle thrushes and
woodpeckers can be seen along this rue.

A shallow chalk quarry will appear beyond
the hedge to your right. There should be many
downland flowers here, such as bird's foot trefoil,
but locals from Leigh Park have used it as a cycle
track and burnt offerings of illicit transport have
degraded the site. At the far end of the quarry
is a substantial barrier of tyres. After this, turn
sharply left to leave the lane by an old beech
tree and pass over a stile south along Staunton
Way. There's a nice replanted hedge along your
way here as you amble downhill, with trains
bleating warning. After 1,500 m you'll come to a
byroad, by an old sycamore favoured by a green
woodpecker.

Cross this road over the stile, turn right along the hedge and make your way into St Hubert's Church – this is small and Saxon, calmly cheerful and famous within the Society of Antiquaries for its 1330 medieval wall paintings, which show biblical scenes – Salome performing a sword dance, and the hairy anchorite who seduced women and as penance had to walk on all fours thereafter, among others.

Continuing south-east downhill to the valley bottom, turn sharply left, north-east between a downland slope on your right and a field on your left. When you come to the byroad again, turn half-right up a slope and into the woods. Stay on the wide forest ride uphill after some steps, walking almost east through the dense yew and ash forest.

At the hilltop you pass into Sussex again, but turn sharply right (no arrows) and walk uphill until you see a muddy path to your left. Take the left blue arrow route downhill again, under some overhead cables, coming out into the fields and to the starting point, where I see a vision of the Morris as white as the chalk fields and more than ready to go home for tea.

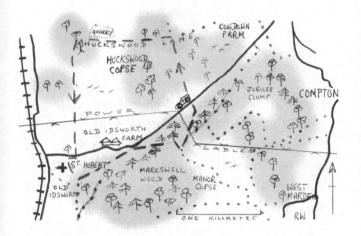

Rewell Wood

This walk of 7 km (4.4 miles) runs through heath and woodland, almost to Arundel.

Parking is available on the roadside in the generous lay-bys on the A29 at **Fairmile Bottom** (SU991096). The footpath leads up a slope to **Yewtree Gate**, from a small lay-by next to the site of the old cafe, now demolished. This is a steep climb, past ancient leaning beech trees, yews and ash. At the top, pass Yew Tree Gate, crossing various tracks, to come out into open scrubby heathland, recently cleared of trees where gorse, rush, wood-sage and bramble provide a habitat for nightjars, hobby falcons and stonechats in summer. Cross the gravel road on the bend and continue south-east, with a mature larch on your right. This is **Sherwood Rough**, once a prehistoric settlement.

Next, head downhill with the old pond on your left and the beginnings of some open downland on your right, with marjoram and dogwood. Walk uphill again into a neglected Scots pine plantation and to a young beech, badly damaged by grey squirrels. Forestry Commission notices here indicate intentions of new eco-friendly management. The ancient boundary bank on your right grows old yews, beech and oaks. Head downhill again past broadwood trees planted in plastic tubes and join the vehicle track. The north edge of **Arundel Park** now begins to show itself to the right, with rising valley grassland – stay with the vehicle track on the yellow arrow route. Look out for a good seat made of horse chestnut trunks, where you can stop for rest or refreshment. Looking ahead, you can see the thin spire of Arundel. Within 120 m of the A284, turn sharply right at the fingerpost, leading between wire fences. Follow this into the deep, damp, gloomy wood to **Park Bottom Barn**, where ivy and ferns grow in abundance.

Climb out on the yellow arrow route, ignoring the purple arrow to your left. At the top of the rise, cross the stile, then turn sharply right, almost doubling back north-west along the edge of the wood – note the roe deer browse-line along the ivy. Turn left at the old wood gate barring your path, through a small metal bridle gate, heading west, into meadows, following frail-looking fingerposts – the noisy A27 will be on your left. Stay on the track to Rewell House, aiming just left of the grey steel barn. You'll catch a glimmer of the sea far to your left if you're lucky. Enter the wood, keeping the house to your left, by an abandoned cultivator. Keep heading north-west, crossing various rides, including an eight-crossway in the centre of Rewell Wood. Eventually this track splits: take the blue arrow route on the right, soon to plunge steeply downhill back into Fairmile. Though the bridleway now goes down to the road, it is more pleasant to walk along the grassland slope of the nature reserve back to the lay-bys, where English longhorn cattle sometimes graze and browse, looking as ancient and white as the Morris.

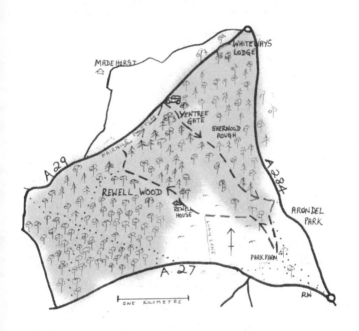

ONE KILOMETRE

Slindon Wood

Slindon Wood was knocked sideways by the hurricane of 16 October 1987 – so let's wander for 3 km (1.8 miles) to see what it's like today.

There are several parking areas around this famous beauty spot; I often use the one at the north end, at SU952085. Most of the paths on this walk are hard, dry and made of gravel. Entering the wood to walk south-east you might say to yourself: 'Hurricane? What hurricane?' The beeches here are enormous, tall and straight. So are the oaks and the young sycamores, although after a while you'll begin to see an elephants' graveyard. Some of the old oak hulks are still alive, but with twenty-year-old branches coming out of their sides. The woodpeckers and nuthatches just love this place and spindle bushes and honeysuckle abound here, too. Tracks come in from the left, but just keep walking south, to the right. This area is also a graveyard for what were once the chalk downs, millions of years ago. All that's left are the flints – zillions and zillions of them.

At a crossroads, where you should keep right, notice an old female yew tree with berries. If you look under her skirts you will see she is making a new family of clones by laying down her branches on the ground where they take root, forming new trees. This seems to be a trysting place for wood spirits, too. Old plantings of spruce and pine give a fragrance to the air, as does the damp bracken and leaf mould. Turn sharply left, at the alternative car park near the A27, and head uphill into a silver birch grove. Some beech replantings have been badly damaged by grey squirrels, curse them.

At this point you should start your return north by going left at minor junctions. Root plates can be spotted everywhere from now on, showing how many trees were lost. The walk opens out into pleasant glades of grass and bramble bushes, and then comes to a fine cambered flint track – there are various seats along this way for your picnics. Around you are battered beeches like Fountains Abbey ruins, but farther on is a remarkable untouched beech forest, with magnificent high trunks and branches like the fan vaulting in Salisbury Cathedral. Notice the old **Slindon Park** earth bank, built to hold deer in centuries past. At the hidden pond on your right, with **Keeper Cottage**, turn left onto the muddy path, wandering back to your start point. I find my Morris, which was almost crushed to death in 1987 on that frightening night of mighty wind in the woods where I live.

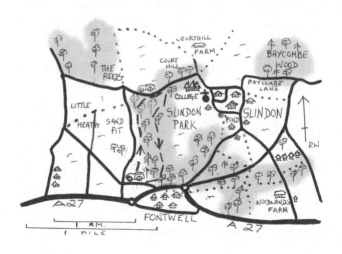

Sutton &
Bignor Park

This walk of 4 km (2.5 miles) is through one of the most secret and ancient parts of Sussex I know.

Parking can be found at **Barlavington Estate's Lord's Piece** car park, on the road between Fittleworth and Watersfield at SU993169. First, find the bridleway south-west into the woods – here is an antique landscape of hoary oaks, black mud, swamps and ditches; marsh tits, chiffchaffs and woodpeckers abound. Also, hemlock, water dropwort, alders and lords and ladies can be spotted; it is one of the most curious landscapes I have ever been in; it is gothic and would be sombre if it were not for the abundant wildlife. Every tree has a face, a medieval gargoyle, with epicormic growths. This is the land of Puck and Kipling's last-century creation – wilderness at its most Romantic. If you don't feel the resonances of distant time do not bother with this walk, because you'll only see the black mud.

After a while, the spagnum and birch swamp turns to silver sand, with a bracken hill to the left, a rush swamp to the right, and thick blackthorn hedges around. You'll arrive at Keyzaston Farm, with its graveyard of ploughs, cultivators and cattle crushes. Turn left onto the Sutton road and continue for 150 m, with a view ahead of Barlavington Down. Go left on the yellow arrow route over the stile at Tudor Cottage, taking the footpath running behind their garden. Here join the Literary Trail to cross another stile into some meadows, eventually coming to Winters Copse, and follow the edge of this. After another stile the path splits: take the left path and continue to follow the woodland round to the left, where you join up with Hospital Copse and The Swares wood, which comes in from the right.

Now the path dives down to a stream, with a heavy plank bridge next to a poled horse jump; this makes a good place to sit for lunch, with the possibility of seeing a bullhead in the stream, as I have. A beautiful bluebell wood, too. The path then climbs out and curves right, passing the rusty chassis of a very old, heavy vehicle (I could not make out what it had once been). Continue through the gorse brakes, bisected for pheasant shooting, eventually arriving at a crossroads. Here turn left onto the bridleway, which runs by another Sussex shaw, along which many Turkey oaks are growing; in the woods to the right was once an old duck decoy. On entering Decoy Copse, keep right as the bridleway splits and follow the track through the laurel wood. At the stream crossing, note golden saxifrage growing on edges of the water. Arriving at the road, turn left. Here I return to the Morris, a mere 500 m away. When I get in, its springs stridulate like the field crickets nearby on Lord's Piece.

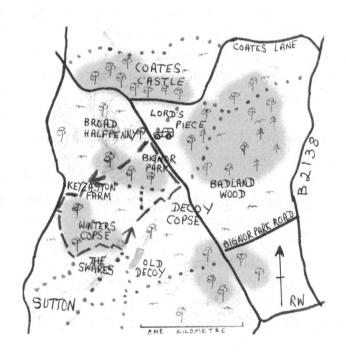

COATES LANE

COATES CASTLE

LORD'S PIECE

BROAD HALFPENNY

BIGNOR PARK

BADLAND WOOD

KEYZASTON FARM

DECOY COPSE

WINTERS COPSE

THE SWARES

OLD DECOY

SUTTON

BIGNOR PARK ROAD

B 2138

RW

ONE KILOMETRE

The Severals

Only a mile west of Midhurst is the Severals Wood, a place well known for its bird life; this is a pleasant stroll of 2.5 km (1.5 miles) under its pine woods.

In the car, head for a small lay-by at SU869207, on the minor Severals Road running south off the A272, but beware the very sharp turn if coming from Midhurst as you enter this minor road. The parking bay, for three cars, is almost 300 m from main road. From here walk west on the white arrow route – this track is also the **Serpent Trail.** Along the way you'll see masses of Scots pines, some birch and some rhododendron, which in early June have heavy blossom – mind the roots crossing your path, which will trip the unwary. Grey squirrels may be peeling cones, and even biting off unripe green cones, and scattering the bits on your path. Note a few plants of ling and an occasional dense white patch of heath bedstraw along the edge of the path – not very common.

After 500 m turn sharply left, still on the white arrow route. Soon you'll arrive at an open area of cleared forest, overlooked by a deer-stalkers' hide – this should be a natural habitat for nightjars. These birds – big moth-catchers related to the swifts – will make a loud reeling noise like crickets at around 9.30 p.m. each summer evening. Note the patches of Yorkshire fog grass and sweet vernal grass at the track junction, where the Serpent Trail goes off west – you should continue south, keeping to the cleared area to your left. Take note of the splendid honeysuckle here, which is the foodplant of the white admiral butterfly's caterpillar – these big black-and-white butterflies should be here in July. There is one small broom bush here, too.

Birds throughout this woodland include great spotted woodpeckers, wrens, blackbirds, chaffinches and chiffchaffs. Look out for climbing corydalis entwined among plants here, too. Next, cross over the tracks, taking the yellow arrow route: this leads into a dense, damp woodland with hidden soggy pits. Turn right on the next yellow arrow, were you'll find the path begins to circle left, and finally east-south-east. Look down for clumps of densely tufted remote sedge (*Carex remota*) growing low along this muddy path. Turn left next, onto the white arrow route, and head northward for the next 800 m. You will pass over two cross-tracks, as well as a 'Mellor's shed' (remember your *Lady Chatterley's Lover*), in which wrens now roost, and a grey squirrel has vented frustration on the interior. Then come to a five-crossway, where you should turn right to take the white arrow route. This brings you back to the Severals Road, where you turn left and walk for 120 m. I head back to Morris, one of several in the Midhurst area.

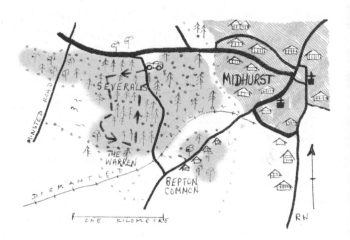

West Dean Woods

This walk is best taken in spring to see one of the most famous wild daffodil colonies in the south: they are usually at their peak around 15 March. The area is owned by West Dean Estate (The Edward James Foundation) and the reserve managed by the Sussex Wildlife Trust. The walk is 4.7 km (2.9 miles).

Parking can be found at the roadside, under old beech trees at SU845153, on the minor road which runs from West Dean (A286) to Chilgrove, about 4 km (2.5 miles) from West Dean and about 2 km (1.2 miles) north-east of Chilgrove. From the car park go west (right) along the road for 100 m where, on the corner, climb down into a sunken lane and turn right (north-east). You will find on your right a large chalk ball: one of a series making a trail over the Downs from Cocking to West Dean, by the environmental sculptor Andy Goldsworthy. Continue up the path past a sign indicating the 40-acre nature reserve on the right (note access is not allowed, except with a permit). Hazel here is coppiced on roughly a seven-year cycle, by volunteers, enabling 300 species of flowering plants to thrive. Oaks, ash, beech and bird cherry have been left as timber standards for maximum biodiversity.

Trackside verges here have a variety of woodland flowers, throughout the spring and summer. Forty-three species of bird breed in these woods, including willow tits, treecreepers, great spotted woodpeckers, marsh tits, chiffchaffs and willow warblers. Look out also for the great variety of butterflies, according to season: in the spring, brimstone and orange-tip; later, speckled woods and silver-washed fritillaries. Soon after you will arrive at a more open area where the wild daffodils grow – the number varies from year to year, as it takes several years for a bulb to mature enough to flower. It is, of course, forbidden to dig up or pick these flowers.

On your left, at the track crossroads, you'll see another Goldsworthy chalk ball – now spectacularly split by frost and snow (weathering was part of the sculptor's intent). Leaving the nature reserve, continue straight on, north, on the ride through a commercial forest. At some large firs, where another chalk ball lies on your right, continue ahead: immediately on your left look out for a wide but shallow Bronze Age tumulus, rather hidden under the trees. Continue north for 300 m, when you should turn sharply left, south-west, and continue downhill – note the regular banks, about every 50 m, which were Bronze/Iron Age/Roman farm field boundaries. Listen out for goldcrests singing in treetops.

Eventually you'll reach **Sandy's Bottom** and a five-crossways: stay ahead on the wide valley track, surrounded by some quite magnificent, very tall fir trees, until you reach the road where you should turn left. Coming to (and passing) **Staple Ash Farm** on your left, keep on walking uphill, where you'll spot another chalk ball on the corner, and continue on the road under the mature trees at first, then round the bend and back to beginning. I, as ever, to the Morris, which fortunately isn't quite as static as those chalk balls.

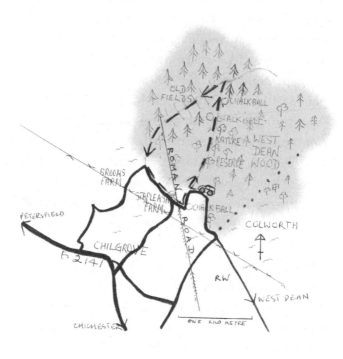

Wispers Copse

Here is a Wealden walk of 4.5 km (2.8 miles) to hear spring birdsong in damp woodlands. The word 'Wispers' derives from the Norman usage '*wysps*', described in forest rolls, meaning small thickets of trees where 'wisps' of branches (and hay) could be taken.

A car park can be found at SU864254 on Linch Road, Woolbeding Common, 3.5 km (2 miles) north-west of Midhurst. Exit the car park heading south-west, ignoring the path that appears to your right (west) as you travel downhill, with wonderful views to Rake. Continue over the cross-paths to reach Woodhouse Farm, following the blue arrows that take you left. Note the enormous sycamores, limes, oaks and horse chestnuts here, where you may hear green woodpeckers yaffling and great spotted woodpeckers drumming. In season, chiffchaffs and blackcap warblers can be heard singing together with mistle thrushes, song thrushes, blackbirds, wrens, chaffinches, great tits and marsh tits.

Eventually you will come to a small lake, probably an old hammer pond, where private anglers contemplate carp – you may see moorhens and a pair of little grebes. The three species of duck that are sometimes seen on this and similar ponds hereabouts are tufted duck, black with a white flank, pochard, chestnut head with grey flank, and wood duck, a colourful introduction from America, but now feral in parts of England. Ignore the footpath going left uphill and continue south-west for another 500 m, to a diagonal right yellow arrow route that brings you immediately to a small house. Here, turn north on a right-handed route around the house, and head back along the side of the valley. A buttressed ancient wall stops pollarded beech, with their fantastic shapes, tumbling into the sandy gully.

You will then enter Oakham Common: stay on the green arrow route, keeping right, and turn right again at the junctions. You'll spot Scots pine here and also a strange old oak tree standing as if on stilts – its roots have had the sand washed from under them. Water springs onto the house road: look for the yellow arrow route going right into a birch and a rhododendron grove, which is part of Wispers Copse. **Stedham Marsh** lies to your left – it's a very soggy place, but you have a sort of raised causeway to walk on. Take the left footpath at the fingerpost through an area which is what Ploegsteert Wood now looks like on the old World War One battlefields. This is a good place to see white admiral butterflies, after they emerge from chrysalis hidden in wild honeysuckle in July. (The old name for this butterfly was 'admirable white' – and red admiral was 'admirable red' – nothing to do with the navy!)

From here keep heading south-east, uphill through the young bracken, eventually appearing on the path that leads you back to the car park and, for me, the old white Morris – or should that be the White Admiral, since every July it emerges fresh from another MOT: certainly it is an admirable white Morris!

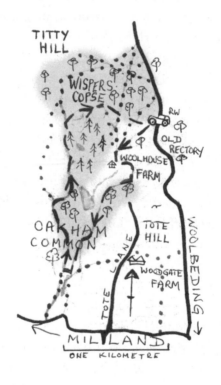

Village
Walks

Colworth Down

Here is a farm and forest walk of 7.5 km (4.8 miles), mainly along country lanes.

Take the A286 to West Dean village, turning north-west at the school opposite the Selsey Arms, and drive under the railway bridge and continue about 3 km (2 miles) to park at the roadside at SU846147, at the junction of Hylters Lane (one can also approach from the Petersfield road, the B2141, turning at Brickkiln Farm and continuing for about 1 km until arriving at the same place). There is also a bus stop in West Dean village, on the A286 near the school.

If you've parked at the bottom of Hylters Lane, proceed along the cinder track (so-called because cinders from Wales were brought here in Edwardian times to make the road fit for royal shooting parties) north-east, with the forest on your left and the wonderful open farm fields to your right. After 750 m turn right onto the bridleway down to Colworth Barn, now a private house. 'Colworth' derives from the Saxon settlement of 'Cula'. Note the fine field maples in the hedge here – the area is a hunting ground (in winter) for the occasional hen harrier, with buzzards and red kites all year. It's a fine place to see flocks of finches in the winter, too.

Climb out to Colworth Farm to join the road running southwards to West Dean village – this is a deep, quiet road more like those of the Weald. In spring it is alive with birdsong from around thirty species; in autumn note the often large parties of titmice, often with five species banding together. Pass under the old railway arch, which carried the line from Chichester to Midhurst, and you'll arrive at the A286, opposite the driveway into West Dean College. (Buses stop here from both Chichester and Midhurst, so this is an alternative start/ finish point to the walk.) Turn right and walk along the pavement. Once opposite the Selsey

Arms pub, turn right at the school, passing again under the old railway line. (If you want refreshment, turn left at the Selsey Arms and find the very friendly village store, where teas, etc. are available.)

Walk north-west now, following the road. This part of West Dean is known as the Warren, due to ancient rabbit warren enclosure where the animals were farmed – a very lucrative trade at one time. The woods here are plantations over an old hazel coppice, with oak and beech. Climbing to Lodge Hill through the sharp bends, the view once more expands wonderfully. Also, this is a good place to see wintering brambling and chaffinch flocks, buzzards and red kites. The long, straight walk down is flanked by a young linear beech strip, which is very colourful in the autumn. Note the Andy Goldsworthy chalk ball sculpture here, one of many on a local trail, some bigger, but not so well shaped as my ancient Morris Minor and not so useful.

East Marden

There is a puzzle in the Mardens, as I shall reveal. The walk here is 4.5 km (2.8 miles).

Parking can be found just off the B2141, the Chilgrove–South Harting road (SU814147). Turn left at the top of the hill out of Chilgrove on the East Marden road, where immediately you'll see a lay-by opposite **Hill Barn** private road. This hilltop is a good place to hear skylarks and see red kites, breeding nearby in recent years. Walk down the hill on the road, enjoying the view to your right of Harting Hill and the chalk turf bank with yews, left of East Marden Down. The village here is famous for its thatched well-head at the central crossways – as you approach you'll see **St Peter's Church** to your right: although largely thirteenth century, its simplicity was swept away rather by the more sentimental Victorians. Amazingly, the church is home to the tiny golden-piped organ, once played by Prince Albert when it was at St James' Palace in London. The modern church kneelers are bright and good, with those at the altar rail depicting local wildlife.

Continue on the right-hand road north-west, noting first a male yew then a female in the church boundary – where there are rooks raucously clamouring in the tall trees. Follow the road for 400 m and, at the sharp bend, go straight ahead into the fields, keeping just right of the wire fence. Ahead you will see an ashwood hanger on a scarp slope called **Battines Hill Wood**; to the right are the slopes of **Apple Down**. Keep half-right on the yellow arrow route, which passes a rusty water tank on stilts and a 250-year-old ash, and continue north-west across the field, gradually leaving the holly/hazel/elder rue to your left as you go. Find the stile crossing the next rue: you now enter the puzzle.

Before climbing Apple Down, note the strange geological feature formed in the Ice Age which you are to cross: this is a depression into which, as the Ice Age ended, melted water must have collected, with no immediate stream outlet. Textbooks tell us that the Mardens took their name from Saxon chronicle *'Meredone'*, which meant 'Boundary Hill'. But scholars admit the difficulty in distinguishing the ancient word *'maere'*, meaning boundary, from the word that also meant *'mere'* (as in lake). All the Mardens surround this depression; so it would seem that, possibly, this whole flat valley towards Stoughton was once a lake.

The puzzle aside, continue the walk by climbing across the downland, over the stile at the road, where you should turn right. At the junction turn right into Long Lane. The view south here shows the two bell barrows overseeing Kingley Vale. Continue on Long Lane to the sharp right bend, where you should continue straight ahead through a hazel tunnel, which will bring you out onto the main Chichester–Petersfield road (B2141), with a view out over the valley to the north-east (you may get a soaring red kite sighting here). Turn right (south) along the road, keeping to the wide grass verge, and after 150 m turn right again on a sharp bend, following the yellow arrow route across the (cereal) field to the beginning. Here I return to a 'mere' Morris, not drowning but waving.

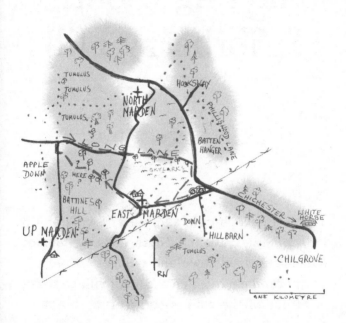

Harting (South) & Torberry Hill

This is a pub, church, and literary walk of 4.3 km (2.7 miles) around South Harting, one of our most prized downland villages.

Cars can be parked on the main village street or at one of the pubs – the White Hart or the Ship, both of which are timbered and friendly (SU785195). So, too, the Church of St Mary & St Gabriel, nearby, with the magnificent Elizabethan roof timbers sporting ornamental pendants. Make friends here with three Elizabethans in ruffs and scarlet tunics, lounging on their tomb, and the super modern kneelers showing village history and wildlife. The vast walled churchyard is worth a visit, too, with its railed enclave for the Fetherstonehaugh (Fanshaw) family – there are also lots of cheap and useful postcards for sale to help church funds.

Outside, don't miss the famous Eric Gill war memorial. Now walk north past the pubs, noting the 1887 Jubilee water pump next to the old village school, complete with symmetrical windows and spikey bargeboarded gables. Keeping the Ship to port, sail north along North Lane and, after 700 m, at the left road junction, find the big white house, in which the writer Anthony Trollope lived from 1880– 82. Continue north for another 250 m, finding the yellow arrow route going left over a stile and into some meadows – note two splendidly straight Scots pines here. The footpath puts you out onto a road after 600 m, near a tumble of old tractors in Torberry Copse. Turn right here to follow the country road, but keep left at the two road junctions you will soon meet. Here you are circling a little mountain, which has on its peak two circular Iron Age hill forts from both 500 BC and also 100 BC; they are part of a chain of forts that include Cissbury, Trundle, Old Winchester and St Catherine's. Torberry is Old English: *'torr byrig'* means 'hill fort'.

At the second road junction, where an old bottle pit is just visible in the undergrowth, look for the Sussex Border Path sign leading up to left, off the road and into the wood – follow this for 800 m southwards. You will pass a mammoth beech tree with a girth I have estimated at 7.5 m. The woodland here is very pleasant, with bluebells in spring and lots of birds such as marsh tits, great spotted woodpeckers and nuthatches. Reaching the main Petersfield road, turn left, taking in the fine view of South Harting, with its copper-green church spire nestling beneath the shoulders of the downs, smooth as the contours of the old Morris Minor. Look for the footpath to the church off the road, via Church Farm, 650 m down the road, and take a final look at those Elizabethan loungers before wending your way home.

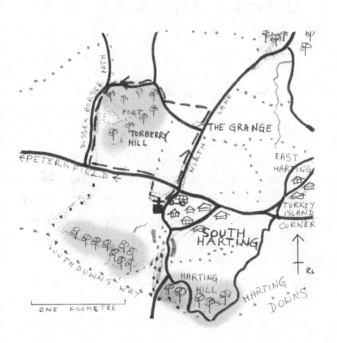

Harting Combe

The distance of this walk is 6.2 km (3.9 miles), much of it on the Serpent Trail (there is some rough walking included – 'combe' means 'steep' – so strong boots are recommended). Wood duck, goldcrests, caverns, gullies and ghylls with brooding pine forests are the highlights of this walk over the greensand of Harting Combe.

Parking can be found about 1.5 km north of Rogate, on the Rake–Borden road in the Forestry Commission car park at SU809254 From here proceed north-west along the ride next to the road: in the summer this shows you bell heather and the rare lesser gorse, which has tiny prickles; European gorse is the more familiar, larger spiny stuff. Soon you'll see a turning right (north-easterly) on the blue arrow route, heading steeply downhill. Here is geology reshaping the land under your feet, so take care.

Streamlets and sometimes torrents gush downwards here, even drowning the barely audible songs of Britain's smallest birds, the goldcrests and firecrests, high in the pine canopy. This is also the land of the well-named cloudberry bush, which thrives in these damp extremes. On hot summer days the smell of turpentine invigorates as you breathe in what the pines breathe out. The path zigzags around and crosses some funny little old bridges that may keep your feet dry in the winter. At the road turn right, but now watch out for a different sort of danger: this is rich man's country and they are used to having right of way in their posh cars.

After 350 m, you'll come to a stile on your left side in the hedge, with a yellow arrow pointing north across a grass field. This path enters birch and alder woods and soon you will see Combe Pond appearing through the trees. I have seen wood duck (Carolinas) here, an unusual American species – the male's plumage is purple, buff, black, white and with rainbow iridescence. There are also tufted duck and pochard, mallard, moorhens and coots. Little grebes also breed in the summer among the water lilies. The footpath comes out at Pond Bay onto the road; here turn right to follow the road, turning right again at the junction, walking on for a mile, then looking for the yellow arrow route post near some white gates, which will take you left (south) uphill through the wood.

Ignore all paths leading left: they will take you to Borden or Trotton Marsh – stay right, proceeding southerly. After nearly 1 km of uphill slog (you are returning roughly parallel to the outward downhill path) you come to the top of the road, where you should turn right and walk for 750 m back north-west to the car park – I to the Morris, sulking slightly at the sight of all those glamorous Euroboxes with shining paint and potential computer problems. Don't worry, old girl, I say, you have only broken down once in thirty years and I was soon able to put you right again. We've both got plenty of working life left.

Afterword

Sadly, since these walks were undertaken, the faithful white Morris Traveller I so loved has died of old age. However, this has meant that my even more trusty, faithful (and older) Alvis TA 14 Shooting Brake now undertakes the transportation duties, ensuring there will be many more walking adventures to come!

Acknowledgements

With thanks to our subscribers:

Tyrone Anderson
Sally Arnhold
Jacqueline and Barry Arnold
John and Philippa Arnott
A. F. and P. A. Bailey
John Baker
M. J. D. Baker
Andrew Berriman
William and Christine Bodey
Bognor Regis W.I.
Sheila Brading
Michael Colbourne
Gerald Gresham Cooke
Nicholas Corkery
Peter Cornell
Susan Cross
John Davies

Roger Davis
Mrs Monica Day
Kate Devane
Anna Drynan
Kay Everrett
L. Fitzgerald
Susan Flynn
Barry Fox
Mrs E. B. Froud
Stuart Graham
Susan Griggs
Sarah Gunn
Jackie Haggis
M. T. M. Hannant
Jonathan and Catherine Harry
Pamela Hockley
Mrs Gay Hodgson

Jane Honeybourne
Mrs J. D. Hunting
Mrs Philippa Jackson
Ursula Jackson
Mike and Jacki Kingsford
Anna Liebschner
Krzysztof Maczewski
Janet Marr
Stella Martin
Mr T. G. May
Duncan McNicol
Derek Morgan
Vivienne and Les New
Wendy Oakland
P. Outrim
Margaret Page
Mrs P. Payne
Sue Payne
Mrs Julie Peverett

Mrs R. F. Pitts
Mrs D. E. Pollard
Margaret Porter
Jackie Robinson
Bubbles Simmonds
Linda Smith
Pam and Ken Smith
Sam St Clair-Ford
Benjamin Stefanski
Paul Stefanski
Richard Stefanski
John Templeton
Paul Vincent
Robert Walker
Anne and Jeremy Whitman
Mrs Brenda Wild
Mrs U. Wild
Mrs P. de RL Williams

THE
BIG WALKS
OF GREAT BRITAIN

including South Downs Way, Offa's Dyke Path, The Thames Path,
The Peddars Way and Norfolk Coast Path,
The Wolds Way, The Pembrokeshire Coast Path,
The West Highland Way, The Pennine Way

DAVID BATHURST

The Big Walks of Great Britain

David Bathurst

£9.99   ISBN: 978-1-84024-566-0

From the South Downs Way to Offa's Dyke, from the Thames Path to the Norfolk Coast Path, from Pembrokeshire to the West Highlands, there are big walks here to keep you rambling all year round. And what better way to discover the landscapes of Great Britain, from green and gentle dales to majestic mountains and rugged cliffs?

An indefatigable walker, David Bathurst has unlaced his boots to produce this invaluable companion to the fifteen best-loved long-distance footpaths of Great Britain. His appreciation of the beauty and history of the British countryside and his light-hearted style will appeal to novice and experienced walkers alike.

This comprehensive guide to the best big walks offers detailed descriptions of the trails and a wealth of geographical, historical and practical information, including route maps and places of interest along the way.

The Walker's Friend

A Miscellany of Wit and Wisdom

Jude Palmer

The Walker's Friend

A Miscellany of Wit and Wisdom

Jude Palmer

£9.99   ISBN: 978-1-84953-052-1

'I have two doctors, my left leg and my right'
G. M. Trevelyan

As Henry David Thoreau said, an early morning walk is a blessing for the whole day – a time to breathe fresh air and feel the grass under your feet, replenish the spirits and calm the mind, and let the thoughts flow while enjoying nature's bounteous pleasures.

Hikers, ramblers, dog walkers and casual strollers will savour this beautifully designed collection of quotations and excerpts from classic and contemporary writing, both humorous and evocative, interspersed with practical tips on everything from walking boots to where to spot wildlife.

Have you enjoyed this book?

If so, why not write a review on your
favourite website?
Thanks very much for buying this
Summersdale book.

www.summersdale.com